The Rookie's Guide to Getting Published

survival tips from the trenches

Kurt W. Bubna
Jeff S. Kennedy

Essential Life Press
vital resources for the christian life

It's crazy and scary when you're embarking on a book project. But Bubna and Kennedy not only hold your hands through the process with intelligence and hard-won advice, but they cheer for you too. For those journeying on the publication process for the first time, this book is a must.

~ **Mary DeMuth**
author / 30 books including *The 11 Secrets of Getting Published*

This book leaks awesome sauce for rookie writers like me!
~ **Chuck Tate**
Lead Pastor of RockChurch, Peoria, IL
author / *41 Will Come* (forthcoming, Tyndale)

The Rookie's Guide to Getting Published is a wellspring for anyone lost in the desert of book publishing. Why make the fatal mistakes of most first-timers when there is a resource to save you the embarrassment? I highly recommend this guide for anyone looking to make a stellar first impression.

~ **Kimberly Shumate**
agent / Living Word Literary Agency

Writing a book may be the hardest thing you've ever done—until you seek to be published. Fortunately, you're about to read a short yet thorough book that shines ample light on the oftentimes hidden world of publishing. *The Rookie's Guide* is an invaluable resource to help your hard-won words find an audience.

~ **Blake Atwood**
editor / EditFor.me
author / *The Gospel According to Breaking Bad* and *Don't Fear the Reaper: Why Every Author Needs an Editor*

If ever you've had a desire to author a book, spend the next twenty-four hours devouring every page and highlighting every tip in *The Rookie's Guide to Getting Published*!

~ **Cherie Lowe**

author / *Slaying the Debt Dragon: How One Family Conquered Their Money Monster and Found an Inspired Happily Ever After* / author of the popular blog Queen of Free

I wrote this because Kurt asked (see pg. 88)! Rookies fear asking. Asking for help, guidance and support is humbling and risky but like Kurt and Jeff say in this brilliant little book (which I intend to promote and share like crazy) "don't ask and the answer will always be no." I've written six books, five traditionally and one self and I can say without equivocation that Jeff and Kurt are not lying. The first question I ask when someone tells me they have a book idea is "do you care if anyone else knows about it?" Sounds like an insult doesn't it? But some geniuses literally don't care. Van Gogh painted but his ancestors got the check. If that's cool with you—ignore this book.

~ **Jim Henderson**

author / *Jim and Casper Go to Church* and *Question Mark: Why the Church Welcomes Bullies and How to Stop it*
President of Jim Henderson Presents

essentialifepress.org
Essential Life Press
15303 E Sprague Ave, STE A
Spokane Valley, WA 99037.
EssentiaLifePress.org
This book may be ordered online at essentialifepress.org, amazon.com, barnesandnoble.com or wherever books are sold.

Visit the author's websites at
(Kurt) **Kurtbubna.com** and
(Dr. Jeff) **FearlessConversations.net**

ISBN-10: 0990902250
ISBN-13:978-0-9909022-5-6
Edition

2   3   4   5   6   7   8   9   10

CONTENTS

ACKNOWLEDGEMENTS

We want to thank the many friends, family, agents, publishers, editors and publicists that we've been privileged to work with. This book would not exist without them.

INTRODUCTION

CHANCES ARE, you downloaded or purchased this book because you're a writer who wants to be an author—a *published* author. And chances are you have the itch to write because you read something that inspired you and thought, "I could do that. I think I could be an author." I'm also willing to bet that your first love is *writing* and not necessarily all the other stuff that comes along with it.

You *are a writer* and you want to be a published *author*.[1]

But the trouble is that publishers aren't only looking for writers. They want authors who are media savvy marketers—*relentless* self-promoters who work as hard at building an audience as they do at honing the craft. Not only that, but no publisher is going to take the time to educate you about the process of publishing.

When you pitch your idea to editors and literary agents they will have one bottom line: "Is this person ready to launch?" And the answer to that question will determine

---

[1] Jeff Goins, *You Are a Writer: So Start Acting Like One* (Tribe Press, 2012)

1

whether or not you move forward in the publishing process. Being published is a privilege and a huge responsibility.

Think about it for a minute. There was a time when most people were illiterate and unable to read or write. Writing was a specialized skill for which only a few privileged people known as "scribes" were trained.

But now?

Most people in the western world are literate. And what's more, there are seemingly endless opportunities for writing and sharing our thoughts with the world.

Whether it's YouTube or WordPress, you and I have multiple channels for self-expression. And if you wanted to, you could toss this book right now, click on CreateSpace.com and publish almost anything you can imagine (at nearly any level of quality). You upload your unedited manuscript and *blam!* in a few days you'll get a fairly decent book for the cost of an ISBN number and shipping.

BRACE YOURSELF

The truth is you don't need a publisher to build an audience, to cultivate a "tribe" or to develop your platform. Almost everything you need to do as an author can and will be done without them.

So why seek a traditional publishing company for your book?

Again, the issue here is not about writing. You *are* a writer, and you have unprecedented outlets for sharing your writing with the world. The real question is, how do you get published with a traditional publishing house?

Well first you need to know that publishing is both a guild and a business. And if you want access then you'll have to learn the tradecraft and become a savvy businessperson. If you choose to go this route, just realize that you'll possibly endure years of creating proposals (more on that in Chapter 2), pitching your manuscript to agents or editors (Chapter 4), developing your audience (Chapter 5), and writing and self-editing your book. Not to mention the personal time and money you'll spend to market yourself.

Going the traditional publishing route also means that you don't mind giving up most of the profit associated with your book. If that sentence hit you like a punch to the face then just take a minute. Let it sink in. The truth is that unless you are a best seller, or unless you figure out how to leverage your book into a speaking or consulting career, you will probably lose money going with a traditional publisher.

Yes, there are some obstacles along the way. But if you're the kind of person who *must* publish or perish then this book is for you. If you're a determined person who believes that in addition to the pursuit of life, liberty and happiness you've been endowed with one other inalienable right—*to be published*—then read on.

SOME SWEAT EQUITY

Kurt and I wrote this guide because we've been where you are. We've gone through this process and have educated ourselves on what to do and what not do when you're trying to get published. We want you to know that you can do it, too, and we want to help. But success will take some sweat equity as you learn from our mistakes and experience. We want your path to publication to be as smooth as possible.

OUR ANGLE

Truth be told, there are already lots of books and e-books on how to get published for you to choose from. Kurt and I have consumed the information in all of them. In fact, it's because we so highly value those other works that we wrote this one. After having gone through the process, we realized that none of them were written from our perspective. We're just two guys who:

- Have been recently published with major publishing houses.
- Aren't industry insiders.
- Have never been editors or CEO's of major publishing companies.

So what   do we have to contribute that all of these folks haven't already?

We've found that these otherwise helpful books were missing certain foundational information that is vital for first-timers. Sometimes authors have what we call the "Curse of Knowledge." Insider knowledge is great and helpful—unless you've been "in the know" for so long that you've forgotten what it's like to be a clean slate. You don't remember what it was like *not* to know.

What we want to do is to give you clear steps to follow and to highlight certain rookie mistakes that you'll want to avoid.

So here's what you'll get from this e-book:

- A first-time author's perspective that is still fresh.
- Specific takeaways for how to survive the process.
- A systematic guide that will help you thrive instead of flounder.
- Much needed encouragement.
- Help in negotiating the often turbulent and frustrating process of publishing.

- Helpful templates including a proposal, marketing plan, a social media survival kit and more.

HAVING SAID ALL THAT...

My question for you is this: *Are you ready to roll up your sleeves and get to work?* Often when I present this material at conferences, I see eyes roll back and heads slump forward. On occasion I even hear someone groan, "Ugh. Really? We have to do all of *this* to get published? No thanks!" Honestly I understand this reaction.

I encounter people at these writing conferences with wonderful stories who have written compelling copy, and I think, "If this person would just put in the effort and go through the steps then something amazing could happen here." These conference participants often fall into one of two groups: those who don't know what to do or those who know what to do but don't want to follow the steps.

Which group would you say you are in at this stage in your writing journey? I want to encourage you to pursue your dream of authoring a book. I hope you take this advice to heart and get after it and show the world what you can do with your God-given talents.

~ Jeff

CHAPTER 1

SO HERE'S THE SECRET

ON A FAIRLY REGULAR BASIS people ask me (Kurt), "What's the secret to getting published?" We all want the special formula.[2] We're pretty sure famous best-selling authors have figured out something only known by a select handful of writers. We buy books (like this one), follow well-known authors on Twitter and Facebook, and attend writing conferences desperate to discover the gems buried in their minds.

Jeff and I don't pretend to know everything, but we can tell you a few extremely important things we've learned along the way. It's our conviction that you can get published, but as Jeff stated in the introduction, it's going to take a lot of hard work and intentionality on your part to get there from here.

Some time ago, I had the privilege of participating in Michael Hyatt's launch team for his writer's bible, "Platform". As a best-selling author, prolific blogger, and former Chairman and CEO of Thomas Nelson Publishers, Hyatt is a publishing genius. To learn from a master about

---

[2] See also Mary Demuth's *11 Secrets to Getting Published*

how to do a book launch was exciting (more on this in chapter five). As a team member, I received an early edition of his masterpiece and access to a select group of really smart people.

I was giddy. I devoured the book and wore out a couple of highlighters in the process. I read his manual for success from cover to cover in less than twenty-four hours. It was inspiring. Now ready to grow my platform and launch my writing career into the stratosphere, I actually created a file of the top ten things I needed to do to thrive as an author. It was glorious.

There was just one problem: I'm no Michael Hyatt. I don't have his skill, knowledge, background, experience or creative ability. It's an excellent book and I learned a lot— don't misunderstand me—but I was a rookie from the backside of nowhere with exactly no publishing experience. I got a bit frustrated attempting to implement all of his strategies because I didn't initially see the kind of results I had hoped for.

Dang it! What do I do now? Hmmm . . . maybe I'll try a few other book launch teams. Over the next year or so, I had the honor of helping Ken Davis, Mary DeMuth, and Ken Blanchard introduce their latest books. Each time I participated in a book launch team, I grew and added a few more tools to my box, but I was like a two-year-old with a skill saw, inexperienced and dangerous.

Despite my frequent cluelessness, I learned some things along the way, and I promise you they're worth your time because I'm sharing as one rookie to another.

SECRET NUMBER ONE:
WRITE FOR THE RIGHT REASONS

There's good news and there's bad news. The good news is anyone can get published and have a book on Amazon. Nowadays, there are multiple paths a writer can take to become a published author. The bad news is most people don't publish at all because they don't know how to go about it.

My journey as a writer was a bit unusual. I actually started my book (*Epic Grace: Chronicles of a Recovering Idiot*, Tyndale) as a journal for my children and grandchildren. After the death of one of my favorite uncles, I realized I had no idea what he had experienced in his life or what he had learned long the way. I also have a songbook and a set of commentaries that once belonged to my great-great grandfather, who in the nineteenth century was a circuit-riding preacher, a postman, and a teacher, yet I have no information about what he learned in his journey either.

So one day I sat down to write some of the stories of my life. I wrote about my failures and some lessons I had learned the hard way. I shared my passions and my deepest convictions. I documented my life because I had a story to share and a desire to leave a legacy.

At first, my journaling was simply an act of love for the generations who would follow in my wake. In the beginning, I had no aspirations of getting published. But all of that began to change when my wife said, "This is really good. I think you should consider getting it published."

Just for the fun of it, I passed along a very rough draft to some friends. Imagine my surprise when they agreed with my wife. In fact, one of them said, "I heard about a writing contest that is part of a conference called *Re:Write*; I think you should enter it."

That's when I got hit by the publishing bug! From that point on, I decided to do *whatever* it took to get my book published. I read lots of books on the topic and subscribed to every writer's blog I could find. I picked the brains of author friends who graciously put up with my frequent questions. One in particular, Ronna Snyder, author of *Hot Flashes from Heaven: Help When Midlife and Menopause Meet*, became a valuable mentor to me. I committed myself to learn, to grow, and to publish.

At the eleventh-hour, I entered the *Re:Write* contest. In

fact, I spent an entire day working on the lengthy book proposal required for entering. When I emailed it off, I remember thinking, *If this doesn't' work, now that I have a pretty good proposal done, I'm going to blitz the publishing world with my idea for a book.* One way or the another, traditionally published or not, my dream and goal was to see my book in print and available in the marketplace.

I was blown away when I won the contest. The prize included a $15,000 check, an agent, and a book contract with Tyndale Momentum. The rest, as they say, is history, and over the past couple of years, my life has radically changed. I still pinch myself on a regular basis just to make sure it hasn't all been a dream.

Know this, however, even before I won the contest, I was hooked on writing and driven to publish. I considered the entire *Re:Write* experience a gift, but win or lose, I knew I had a story to tell, and there was a fire in my belly to share my journey with others.

That's why I write and why I wanted to get published; because I'm a writer with a story that I know will encourage and challenge others. Write because you are a writer and for the right reasons.

SECRET NUMBER TWO:
WRITE WHAT YOU KNOW

If you know me, the last book you'd ever want to read if I wrote it would be a user's guide to home repairs. I am the polar opposite of a fix-it guy. Frankly, I'm a break-it moron who has almost no mechanical ability or manual dexterity. Following directions has never been my forte, especially when someone who speaks English as a second or third language writes them.

Without hesitation, I will pay somebody to fix whatever I've broken or to put together the new BBQ from Ace Hardware. For a guy like me, Ace is awesome. Unlike some hardware and home supply stores, Ace is known for providing helpful advice to novices, like me. I will pay twice as much to buy it there than I might at the local home supply stores. I don't care. Just don't ask me to use a screwdriver or wrench (though I am exceptionally gifted with a hammer; I just beat things into submission).

I have a toilet that has been running for a long time. Yes, I know, it's a waste of water. Yes, I know, it's easy to repair a running toilet (unless you're me). Instead, the last time I was at Ace I bought a new set of guts for my bowl. For weeks, however, the package has sat there on a table in my garage mocking me. One of these days, I'm going to give it a shot, but I dread it because I know how frustrating it will be.

My absolute lack of handyman giftedness would make any book I might write about repairing stuff a comedy rather than a useful how-to manual. However, I have an abundance of experience with the relational challenges of life, so that's what I tend to focus on in my writing.

What about you? What are you good at? What has life taught you? What do you know that might truly benefit others? What do you have a passion about?

Write what you know.

SECRET NUMBER THREE:
WRITE WELL

You may not be the next Maya Angelou or James Patterson, but please don't write like a third-grader (unless you're in third grade). Continually develop your skills as a writer.

I used to suck at spelling. As a kid, I entered a spelling bee. My teacher tried to eliminate me before we ever got started. "Kurt, perhaps you should sit this one out?" As usual, I ignored her and made a complete fool out of myself when I got eliminated in the first round by the word *bouquet*. When you're hooked on phonics, it's spelled *bookay*. Why the heck do you need a *q* and *t* in that stupid word?

Anyhow, my point is, I've grown. Spell check has actually made me a better writer. On a regular basis, at least two other people review my work, a line editor and a copy editor (we'll explain the difference in chapter three). At first, the editing process was painful, but my editors have made me a better writer.

You must work at your craft to succeed. To use an old cliché, "Anything worth doing is worth doing right."

- Take a creative writing or English class.
- Utilize websites such as Grammarly.com
- Befriend a nerd who is anal about commas and semicolons.
- Be intentional about personal development. Growth is imperative.

By the way, this isn't about perfection, but it is about professionalism. Nothing is perfect (the grammar sharks will find mistakes, and I'm sure it will make their day). Perfectionism cripples your creativity, so don't over-think your first draft when it comes to grammar, spelling and syntax.

Not too long ago, an editor pointed out that I often use a passive voice in my writing. In a sentence written in the passive voice, the subject receives the action. Using words like *is*, *am*, *are*, *was*, *were*, *be*, *being*, and *been* followed by a past participle "ed" almost always means you've made the object of an action into the subject of a sentence. At the heart of every good sentence is a strong, precise verb (more on this in Chapter 3.)

At first, I thought she was crazy until I went back and read my manuscript again. For several weeks, this haunted me. Every time I sat down to write I got sucked into a black hole of despair because my creativity felt stunted.

Now I try not to over-analyze as I write. I simply go back and make whatever changes are necessary in my second or third draft.

Speaking of "drafts," no one gets it right the first or perhaps even second time. I suggest dumping your creative thoughts as fast as they come in your first draft, and then go back again (and again) as many times as necessary to clean it up.

Writing is work. Don't be lazy or impatient. And for heaven's sake, don't share it with the world until you've polished your composition.

Why is all of this so critical? Because quality matters, especially to a potential publisher! The truth is that no matter how much you work on everything else you think is important, if you can't write, then you'll never get your foot in the door. Publishers want good clean copy; they don't have the time to teach you how to write.

SECRET NUMBER FOUR:
DISCOVER AND DEVELOP YOUR TRIBE[3]

The master at tribe building is Jeff Goins. (I highly recommend you subscribe to his blog here: http://goinswriter.com/.) The big idea behind discovering and developing your tribe is finding a community of people who care about what you care about. As Goins puts it, "When you stand for something, people will stand for you."

The path to success begins with finding out what excites you and then finding others who are passionate about the same thing. For example, if you love historical non-fiction, then don't write science fiction. And when you publish your book on Lincoln, do everything you can to market it to people just like you.

A tribe still has a lot of variety, but by and large they share common values and beliefs. If you're writing for a Christian audience, your book can't read like a secular, sexy romance novel, and you better watch your language. If you're writing a technical book for engineers about

---

[3] Seth Godin, *Tribes* (New York: Penguin Group, 2008).

building an airplane, you probably won't use the word *stuff* a lot. "When installing the max capacitor thrust mechanism, be sure to use all the stuff in the box." Your audience generally consists of people like you who have an itch that your writing scratches.

What matters to you? What are you passionate about? What are you an expert at? Remember, write what you know and then write for the people you know (people like you).

Publishers expect, in fact, generally require you to have an established community of followers. Why? Because you will be the primary marketer of your book! (More on that in chapter five.) Therefore, a large, established tribe is imperative to obtaining a contract with most publishers. That's why you must make building a community of followers a development priority in your writing career.

THE GREATEST SECRET OF ALL:
SUCCESSFULLY DEFINE SUCCESS

Things change. Cultural passions ebb and flow. What's hot today will almost certainly not be hot a few years from now (does anyone still use a Palm Pilot?). Sometimes you'll write something ahead of its time, and decades may pass before your genius is recognized. Sometimes you'll write something old and worn out and few will care.

Our culture tends to define success in some very obvious ways. You are a success if your book becomes a bestseller or wins an award. In reality, very few people become bestselling authors. Some of the greatest books I've ever read are out of print today and written by men and women you've probably never heard about. So I'd like to define success a bit differently. Success is,

- writing from a place of passion for the benefit of others.
- creating a well-written book worth reading regardless of its sales.
- using your gift with diligence and staying the course no matter what.
- growing and continually developing your tribe and your skills as a writer.
- holding your book in your hand someday soon (regardless of the publisher imprint on the cover).

CONCLUSION

The level of success you'll achieve is determined by how you define success. Our goal in this guide is to encourage you to dream and to equip you to be truly successful.

CHAPTER 2

YOUR FIRST STEPS

I'M A PASTOR, and over the years I (Jeff) have written stacks of sermons. Years ago, I started writing my sermons word for word as I planned to deliver them. I refer to this as "manuscripting" my messages. A few years ago I wrote what I thought was a halfway decent talk, and I sat back in my chair and thought, "This sermon reads like a book chapter." For the next several minutes my synapses began to fire and I had more thoughts . . .

- "I wonder what it takes to write a whole book?"
- "How long is a book anyway? I'm sure I have enough material for it."
- "What kind of books do pastors write?"

These questions rolled around in my head for a couple of days. I tried to think of anyone that I knew who had written a book so that I could ask them questions about the process. But honestly, I couldn't think of a single person.

My brain just wouldn't turn off. I loved writing and editing my talks and now felt inspired to take all of this material and create a new book out of it.

BLUNDERING BEGINNINGS

So that's just what I did. I went to my sermon folder and began to copy and paste material into one file—mashing it all together and dividing it up into individual book chapters.

I gave the document a title and subtitle and hit save. Then it sat in that file folder for six more months while I dreamed of publishing glory. Occasionally, I'd go back to the file and do some revising. I'd adjust some formatting, correct spelling errors, thin out redundancies, make analogies clearer...

But for the most part I had no idea what to do. So I did what any hungry prospective author would do; I turned to the internet. I remember Googling something like, "How to get published."

A RUDE AWAKENING

Well that was the end of *that* dream. After spending a day reading everything—every blog, eBook and web article I could find on the subject of getting published—I came away discouraged. I realized that I couldn't just call up Penguin Books or Thomas Nelson and say, "Hey I've got a great new manuscript that you're going to love" only to hear them respond, "Whew! It's a good thing you called when you did. Please, send us your awesome new book right away."

What I discovered (as some of you have by now) is that the publishing world is fiercely competitive. You'll be lucky to get your foot in the door and land an interview with an editor or some other influential person in the biz. Even if you have the best work ethic, publishing with a traditional press is daunting.

I came to realize that if I was ever going to have a real shot at this, I would have to do at least three things: 1.) learn how to write compelling copy 2.) begin building an extended audience for this material and 3.) create a compelling book proposal in a fairly standardized format. All of these translated into hard work.

In chapter three I'll talk more about the craft of writing and in chapter five we'll help you develop and execute a marketing plan.

In this chapter, we want to zoom in on how to create a compelling book proposal along with some tips on avoiding unnecessary rookie mistakes.

DON'T SEND THE MANUSCRIPT (YET)

Publishers do not want your entire non-fiction manuscript up front.[4] Instead, they want a non-fiction book proposal. The

---

[4] Realize this may be different for fiction.

book proposal is a 15-25 page document that includes a sample of your writing and a business plan that you will create before submitting a completed manuscript. The proposal will make or break you. With effort and skill, you can create a book proposal that will catch the eye of an agent and an editor, which is the first step in moving toward your dream of being published. I strongly recommend you follow my template in the back, and for more help, you can purchase and download Mary Demuth's superb book *Write a Winning Nonfiction Proposal: Land that Book Deal.*[5]

Why do publishers want a book proposal?

- They don't have time to read your entire manuscript. They have piles (often referred to as a "slush pile") of potential manuscripts to wade through, and publishers have a limited number of editors available to slog through the pile.

- A proposal shows a prospective agent or editor that you know how to organize your thoughts and write clean, interesting copy and that you have a direction for the project. The proposal outlines and summarizes your plan for the manuscript and your plan for marketing the book once it published. It includes a cover letter, a synopsis of the book, and a summary of your marketing strategy.

---

[5] You can find Mary's template at MaryDemuth.com or amazon.com.

- The proposal will force you to self-edit. You'll have to keep it concise while holding your reader's interest (more on that in the next chapter).
- The proposal will help you to think through your marketing and sales strategy. Trust me, you will get really creative when you have to bullet list your sales process in this short proposal document.

So what are the elements of a compelling book proposal? Let me briefly explain what you'll need to develop and then I'll touch on some rookie mistakes you'll want to avoid.

ELEMENTS OF A COMPELLING PROPOSAL

With few variations you will need to include these elements (see **Appendix A for a template**).

Cover Page: This page includes the proposed title and your name and contact information.

One-Page Overview: This is your query letter (See **Appendix B**). It's a one-page overview in letter format that contains several critical elements, each in one paragraph:

- A compelling opening paragraph that hooks the reader and draws them into your subject.

- A transitional statement that connects to the reader's need.
- A brief paragraph that introduces your book and includes the title and focus of your book.
- One solid paragraph that states your credentials to write the book (including your training but don't get crazy with this. It's not your resume).
- A final paragraph that provides information on the proposed length of the book (number of words), the amount of the book that is completed, and the length of time it will take you to finish the book.

Target Audience: The next page should cover your target audience. Who are the readers you're trying to connect with? Your target audience page should include:

- The characteristics of your audience. These are vital stats that create a profile of your particular niche audience. Do you have a specific segment of the population that will respond best to the book you're trying to write? Is there an age range of your preferred buyer? Do you have a particular gender in mind? For example, Mom's typically buy books about motherhood and adults do not typically drive the sales of youth fiction. I personally write my nonfiction books for Christian women between the ages of 25-45. That's my target market. What's yours?

- The motivation of your audience. What factors will motivate them to want to buy your book? What problem does your book solve—and *whose problem* is it? Zoom in on that target group. I've seen a lot of proposals in my mentoring sessions at conferences. Almost none of them have a *particular* audience in mind. They are making the rookie mistake of trying to reach everyone in the whole world. But no book does that. I suggest the reason why most proposals fall short is because they really haven't identified with a specific motivation from a specific target audience.

- The competition. You'll want to list three or four books that are similar in subject matter and concept to the one you're proposing to write. Include the title, retail price, and a description (one sentence) describing the contents of that competing book.

Author Bio: The author bio, or the blurb about you as an author, is a half-page paragraph that describes three things: 1.) Who you are, 2.) What credentials you possess for writing the book and 3.) What else you have published (if anything). Don't make the rookie mistake of trying to be cute with this (unless you are super cute). But you shouldn't' also make the mistake of listing your endless educational pedigree either. Make it interesting but keep it on point.

Marketing Plan: Other than your overall concept and your writing talent, this is the single most important section of your proposal. The marketing section is a simple business plan that will show the publisher how you intend to market the book (see Chapter 5 for tips on marketing and Appendix A for a Marketing Plan Template).

Table of Contents: While you are writing the book, you may find yourself creating a very detailed outline. That's great for you. But for the publisher, you'll want to distill your outline down to a simple table of contents. Don't make the rookie mistake of throwing every little subheading into your outline unless you are authoring an academic or scholarly textbook.

Chapter Synopsis: Expand your outline or table of contents into a brief chapter-by-chapter synopsis. Each chapter should be described in one tight paragraph. Do not include all of the story elements or the subheadings. Distill you proposed chapter into its essence. I recommend you include one sentence as an overview, a second sentence to highlight a main story or an illustrative element, and a third and final sentence to capture the main takeaways from that chapter. This will give your editor or agent a good idea of what each chapter will accomplish.

Three Sample Chapters: This is the place where you begin to showcase your writing. If you create a perfect, water-tight proposal and you have a decent platform (audience), it won't matter if you can't write. So make sure these three sample chapters have been buffed and burnished to perfection. Get help, training, and feedback from trusted sources (see Chapter 3).

These are the basic elements of a good proposal. Again, study the template in **Appendix A** at the end of this book. But before we conclude this subject, let me give you some very specific rookie missteps to avoid during this process.

ROOKIE MISTAKES TO AVOID

Don't send the whole book. Again, publishing companies do not want the whole book. Don't send them your entire 60,000 word non-fiction manuscript. They won't read it.

Don't send your first draft. This may sound like a "der" comment, but you'd be surprised how many first drafts I've seen in mentoring sessions at conferences. After you get the proposal finished, instead of hitting "SEND" hit "SAVE" and let the proposal cool for a while. Take a week off from writing. Come back to it with fresh eyes, and I promise you'll see things that need to be changed. Determine that you will turn in a clean well-written document. On the other hand, don't be paralyzed by the quest for perfection. You want to avoid the polar extremes between shoddy work and perfectionism.

Write more than your three sample chapters. The conventional advice states that you shouldn't write the whole book at this point. I disagree. *Do* write the whole book if you can. You want to have a fairly complete draft of the project. I lost my first publishing contract because I had written only six sample chapters. The publisher sent me a contract, and when I read the cover letter—they wanted the book turned around (completed) in 30 days. While this is unusual, I'll never forget the sting of that moment. I had a contract in hand and knew it was impossible for me to write nine more chapters in 30 days. Eventually I got published, but I learned my lesson well. So don't send the whole book to the publisher, but do *write the book* or as much of it as you can. Even if that book gets rejected, you'll still have a nice file of material from which to draw on your next project.

Take criticism constructively. When you get feedback from a professional, and you will, just take it like a man. Put on your big girl panties and accept criticism like a pro. You need the input of others to make your work the best it can be.

Don't get too fancy. One of the biggest mistakes I see people make in this process is that they try to typeset or format the proposal to be fancy so that it will stand out from all the other "vanilla" proposals out there. Embrace this axiom: *Let your writing be the stand-out feature of your proposal.* Concentrate on dazzling your editor with superior writing. Relentlessly cut the fluff. Typesetting will come later. For now, let your writing set you apart from the others. Your proposal needs to be in a standard 8.5 x 11 Word doc, 12 pt., Times New Roman font. Single space the proposal but double space your sample chapters. You may be an unpublished amateur, but you sure as heck don't want to look like one. You want that super snappy pro style. So less is more.

Remain professional. On that note, it is best if you keep a professional tone in your proposal. I remember the time when my literary agent sent my initial proposal back to me to put the entire thing in third person. Instead of saying, "I wrote this book for everyone who has ever thought…" she made me change it to "Jeff has written this book…" Stay professional in style and in tone.

Don't sell other people's books for them. While your proposal will include "competing titles" or "comparative titles," you don't want to unintentionally promote those books. You're not selling the competing titles; you're selling *your* book. Instead, you want to point out the reasons why your book is a welcome addition to this genre.

Don't hype your proposal (it's not a book yet). Never promise the publisher that yours will be the greatest book since the *Purpose Driven Life* or *The Fault in Our Stars*. Only time will tell whether your book will be worthy of greatness. Let your content and the creativity and the clarity of your writing do the talking for you.

Don't "teach" the publisher what a "really good book" is. They are the professionals and as of yet, you are an amateur. If you are lucky enough to have them offer you critique then listen to it. Don't think that *you* are going to show *them* what an awesome book really is. For a summer, I was in negotiations with a large publishing house. They were after my first book, and my agent called to let me know they were definitely interested and would call me soon. I got a call from the senior editor, and he began to tell me all the ways in which they wanted to change my book and make it better. He wanted to break the one book into three, give each book a different title and market them as a series on discipleship. I have to say I wasn't initially thrilled about the idea. However, I was more thrilled about the prospect of signing a three-book deal than I was about keeping my sacred words intact. So I rewrote the entire proposal based on the editor's advice. In the meantime, I had another offer on the table, so I had the luxury of choosing between the two offers. I took his advice and ended up with two really cool versions of my original proposal which gave me more options. Make sure you stay humble and teachable throughout this process.

Target a specific niche. No book appeals to everyone. After my book *Father, Son, and the Other One* went to publication, I was surprised at just how many people have told me that they just don't read books like that. Ouch. When you first hear this from people, it will sting a bit. But get over it. Your book must have a niche market if it is to succeed. And it simply will not appeal to everyone.

Don't claim uniqueness. One-of-a-kind books almost never get published. One of the common mistakes I made early on was thinking my book had to be unique and unheard of in the industry. In the academic world, in which I was already published, you are rewarded for unique contributions to a field, not a rehash of old ideas. But in the nonfiction publishing world old ideas are a good thing. While you will bring a unique perspective or angle to the subject, you will not be able to sell them an idea that doesn't already have a proven market.

Don't hit SEND until you've acquired an agent. Right before I sent my manuscript out, a very wise and experienced person told me over the phone not to do that. He encouraged me to get an agent first. That was one of the best pieces of advice I've ever received. My agent has opened doors that I would never have had access to. Agents know people who otherwise are not going to pay attention to you. Their job is to represent you to a publisher and advocate on your behalf. (See the **Query Letter** in **Appendix B** for a letter template that you can use to query a potential agent).[6]

CONCLUSION

Let's recap the takeaways from this chapter:

- Turn your non-fiction book manuscript into a detailed proposal.
- Include in your proposal a sample of your writing, a concise overview of the project, and a detailed marketing strategy.

---

[6] For a list of agents, go here http://michaelhyatt.com/literary-agents-who-represent-christian-authors.html

- Send a query letter to a literary agent before you send the proposal.
- Avoid the rookie mistakes that will tank your proposal.

In the next chapter we will talk about writing compelling copy. The best proposal, with the most compelling business plan and marketing strategy, isn't going to bring you success if your writing is substandard. In the next chapter, you'll find out how to punch up your writing and where to find valuable resources.

CHAPTER 3

ROOKIE TIPS ON WRITING

YEARS BEFORE I PUBLISHED *Father, Son, and the Other One*, I (Jeff) was so insanely self-conscious about my writing that I just couldn't let anyone read it. I got *Bird-by-Bird* by Anne Lamott and wrecked that book—reading and rereading it. I wrote, um, crappy (not her word) first drafts, and lots of crummy second and third drafts followed. Eventually, I discovered the zen of writing:

There is no writing. There is only re-writing.

I picked up Michael Hyatt's *Write a Winning Non-Fiction Book Proposal* and read my copy of Terry Whalin's *Jumstart Your Publishing Dreams* like it was holy writ.

I also refused to start a blog. Seriously, I was so self-conscious about my writing quality that I wouldn't even share my thoughts in a simple and informal blog (you now can find my personal blog on matters of faith at fearlessconversations.net). I spent two years working on my manuscript before anyone even knew it existed. I wrote, re-wrote, and re-worked the re-writes. I crafted stories, smoothed out transitions, strengthened my points and brutally self-edited my little manuscript.

There came a point when I thought I might be ready for the world to see my masterpiece. The problem was that I was still fairly self-conscious and knew I needed more help.

A COME-TO-JESUS MOMENT

I was not in a hurry and so I hired a professional editor from The Christian Communicator, the manuscript critique service of Susan Osborn. She assigned me a seasoned pro and told me I could send her my proposal for a critique. I worked hard at being humble in my initial email to my assigned editor,

"Thanks for your kind advice and any suggestions would be so appreciated…"

What-ev. The truth? There was a little part of me thinking," Pshh. Man, when she reads this she is going to be blown away! I've got two words to describe it: *world—rocked!*"

I had gone from being impossibly insecure to being secretly self-assured. I knew I had spent years burnishing those hallowed words of mine. I was passionate about my material and was ready to receive *unqualified affirmation.*

About two weeks went by and I didn't hear anything back from this editor. I figured she was so engrossed and captivated by my writing that she just had to reread it as if she were imbibing a fine wine—one sip at a time.

Then I got the email I had been waiting for. It was kindly worded and encouraging. But when I opened the document to read her comments, they devastated me. That manuscript bled crimson everywhere. She critiqued my overall structure, organization of the material, use of perspective, rambling tangents, off-topic detours, bloated chapters, foggy central idea and thesis (etcetera, etcetera).

She didn't just slam me though. She also encouraged me with straightforward and specific feedback about mistakes that I needed to address. She highlighted the strengths of my writing and showed me where to adjust my focus.

UNFLAPPABLE

At first my editor-for-hire's comments crushed me. I couldn't open my computer to write, and I let the manuscript sit for about three months. I was utterly flummoxed. I was tempted to throw in the towel.

Eventually I made one choice, one critical decision that changed me forever. I decided to make every change, line-by-line, that the editor had suggested. I chose to revisit that manuscript, re-write it again, and make it amazing.

I rewrote that book over ten months, cleaned up every conceptual mess, buffed out the dents in my thinking and spackled holes in my logic. I went back and thinned out the distracting voices in my writing. I ditched the "pedantic professor" and dumped the "finger-wagging-prophet-of-truth" persona that came across as harsh in written form. My frustration had transformed into unflappability. No matter what, I was going to get it right this time.

A year after receiving that first critique, I resent the manuscript to my editor-for-hire friend, who was all too eager to assess my progress. She said she would take another look at it and get back to me.

A couple of weeks went by and I got a second critique from this writing coach. To my delight, she responded very favorably. She felt proud of me for taking her advice and reworking the material. She commented, "I was surprised that you came back. After the first critique, most authors don't come back for a second round."

The last thing she told me was, "This is definitely publishable. Now go find an agent and a publisher. But don't hold your breath. Publishing houses aren't typically taking a lot of new authors right now."

If you want to have a shot, if you want your book, your baby, your dream to have any chance of success, then learn the craft. That's the best place to start.

ROOKIE TIPS ON WRITING

Again, the time you spend to create a compelling proposal will be wasted if your writing is substandard. We have to learn the trade. Whether you write an informal blog, work for magazines or journals, or self publish your stuff, it is vital to learn the habits and disciplines of excellent writers. Although I have written scores of sermons over the years, I had developed some terrible habits that weren't going to work for professional writing.

It's the same issue I had when I was learning to play guitar. I was self-taught for many years, and by the time I actually took formal lessons I was a bit of a hot mess. My classical guitar teacher watched me clang around with some cowboy chords, and after a bit he smiled and kindly said, "Jeff. I think we are going to have to start from square one here." He taught me the proper way to hold the neck, and he showed me correct finger placement and strumming techniques. I felt almost as if I were learning the guitar for the first time because I had to undo so many bad habits.

So, whether you've been writing for years or are new at it, I'll share eighteen vital writing tips to help you improve the quality of your copy:

1. **Just Start.** The best way to learn how to write is to start writing something, anything. Start a blog, keep a journal, join a writing critique group, or keep an idea notebook. However you approach it, just start writing something.

2. **Write about what you love.** Kurt already mentioned that you should write "what you know." I agree with this, of course. However, if you're a computer programmer and you hate your day job, then don't write a book about computer programming because your angst for that subject will radiate through your writing. Write what you know *if it's what you love.* You may have a dream of writing about something that you know little about (for now), and your passion for that subject will motivate you to learn enough to write about it. For now be passionate and be intentional. The expertise will follow.

3. **Use your words.** When you begin writing, you'll have a limited knowledge base and vocabulary with which to formulate sentences and paragraphs. As a writer, you'll

start within the limits of your knowledge and skill. That's okay. Just pour words out on the page and punch it up later.

4. **Write narrative prose.** If you're writing a non-fiction book, then include narrative elements even if it's a how-to book. Stories create worlds in people's minds that make cold principles come to life. Now, you don't have to (nor should you) overdo stories. Unless you're writing a memoir, you don't want to write just a string of stories. Few authors can pull that off well. Enhance your bland prose with some narrative content as illustrations of your points. Having said that…

5. **Don't use "illustractions."** Years ago I had preached a message and employed one too many stories, a few of which were off topic. They were interesting stories, but they had nothing to do with my central point. Afterward, my mentor pulled me aside and said, "Jeff. There's a difference between an illustration and an 'illustraction.'" I knew what he was trying to say. Don't distract your hearers or readers with content that doesn't illustrate the point you want to make.

6. **Try poetic prose.** While your non-fiction book might not be poetry, that doesn't mean it can't feel like it from time to time. My favorite authors are Mark Buchanan, Ann Voskamp and N.T. Wright. All of these nonfiction authors write with a certain poetic flare. One of the habits I've developed over the years to enhance my prose is to read some poetry: Walt Whitman or a few pages of Shakespeare's Sonnets before I write my non-fiction book chapter. Why? I'm not writing poetry, and I'm certainly not writing Shakespearean blabbity blah, but I want the beauty and rhythm of good poetry rolling around in my head before I write prose. And on that note...

7. **Find your unique voice.** We all have those author heroes whom we're secretly trying to emulate. Chances are you started this journey because you read a book or an article that inspired you. There's no shame in emulating your faves. My book, for example inspired my ten-year-old son to write his own book. I watched as he poured over the pages of my book and other author favorites, trying to find his own voice. Most of us who aren't literary savants follow a typical pattern in our development.

- **Phase 1: You emulate your faves.** At this stage of our development, our writing is almost entirely derivative of our heroes. Well, we have to start somewhere. For example, when I first began writing, everything I wrote looked like bad C.S. Lewis. Eventually I began to find my own voice. But at first, I was a shameless knockoff. Now you want to be careful not to plagiarize which is to steal someone's words or thoughts without giving them the credit. But mimicking the style and feel of your favorite authors is perfectly okay. And it's perfectly natural when you're first starting out.

- **Phase 2: Acquire your own vibe.** Did you know that there are no two voices that are the same? Voice print technology used to be the stuff of sci-fi, but now it's reality. And it's made possible because every voice resonates at a unique frequency. The truth is, that as you begin to imitate your idols you'll find your own voice naturally. No one has your unique perspective on the world. No one else has your story or your background or your peculiar vibe. The more you write, the more you'll discover your distinctive angle on the world and life.

- **Phase 3: Derivative no more.** Eventually after lots of practice few people will think of you as derivative of someone else. Did you know that one of C.S. Lewis' writing heroes was G.K. Chesterton? Usually when I point that out to someone, they ask, "Who's Chesterton?" Now imagine C.S. Lewis in the 1920's as he imbibed George McDonald and Chesterton thinking that some day he was going to write like these famous authors. I'm sure you would agree that no one thinks of Lewis' books as unoriginal. Eventually, the young Lewis found his own voice. And eventually (with lots of effort), you'll find yours too. So keep learning from the greats and keep writing. But don't be afraid to mimic the style and feel of your favorites.

8. **Learn about the physics of storytelling.** There are universal laws that govern nature such as the law of gravity or thermodynamics. Physics is the scientific discipline that seeks to discover those laws. In the same way, every writer is governed by universal laws of story telling that Larry Brooks calls *Story Physics.*[7] Brooks describes story physics as that set of foundational principles and essences that make every story work. The need to understand the essential principles and the

---

[7] Larry Brooks, *Story Physics: Harnessing the Underlying Forces of Storytelling* (Amazon Digital Services, 2013).

processes that govern successful story telling are not only important for fiction writers but nonfiction writers as well. If you are using any illustrative material for your nonfiction work (and you should be) then you'll have to master these indispensible forces of story telling. You'll want to make sure you've got a clear concept, believable and relatable characters, a dominant theme, and a discernable structure. While there are many other factors that go into effective story craft, these four elements are provide an indispensable foundation.

- **Concept.** Generally speaking, your entire nonfiction book is telling a story. And perhaps the most important aspect of the story you're trying to tell is whether or not the concept is coherent and clear. Many a story has bit it by having a fuzzy overall concept or murky logic. Make sure your concept is watertight and impervious to falsification. Intuitively, every reader will be able to spot elements of your story that can be falsified. Over time, this will lead to an erosion of trust, and the reader will simply put your book down because they have either subconsciously or consciously thought, "This just seems like bull." Or they'll think "Something's off. Something doesn't seem right about this." It's because your core concept isn't bedrock yet. So start with a solid concept. For example, one writer pitched me their idea in a mentoring session about a book based on "friend addiction." The topic sounded intriguing. Before we even made it to the third page of her proposal, I said, "Wait a minute. I'm not getting it. What do you mean that this book will help people solve their 'friend addictions'?" After 10 minutes of listening to the writer's explanation I still wasn't getting it. Her story wasn't connecting with me. The problem is that her core concept was muddled and ill conceived. A solid core concept will ring true with readers. A phony concept will leave people scratching their heads wondering "huh?" So how do you test your concept to make sure it connects? The best way to test a new recipe is to make the dish and feed it to people. So find some friends you can trust who will give you direct feedback on your concept and gauge their reaction. The second best way to ensure you have a solid core concept is to see if it has already been done in other books. Especially successful books. If it has, then you've got a proven core idea that can drive your project.

- **Relatable Characters.** The best stories aren't about things. They're about people. When illustrating your principles, the characters you use have to be believable or at least plausible. It's okay to enhance your characters with a little humorous exaggeration. But if it looks as if every one of your subjects are caricatures of real people, then you're readers won't buy it. Eventually, they'll categorize you as a master of hype. This is particularly true for the "Realize Your Dream" genre. If every success story you trot out is a home run then something will not ring true about those examples because life and success are rarely like that. You can also run the risk of supplying people with false hope. Not even Jesus' Disciples had flawless faith. People want to see the imperfections and the real life struggles of your subjects. They want to see the patina and the wear on your heroes. So how do you ensure your characters are accessible? There are several tests you'll want to apply in nonfiction writing. Is the character relatable? Does this person find himself or herself in a situation or dilemma that is common to the human experience? Does the character react like a real person would? With nonfiction in particular, you'll want to make sure your subjects are either real people, a composite of several real people (maybe create one person who is a combination of several similar traits you've encountered with people in your life), or a parable. Having believable and accessible characters is a universal law of good story telling.

- **Theme.** Your book needs to have one coherent theme. And the details of that story need to contribute to the overall picture you're trying to create. Lots of extraneous details will induce cognitive rabbit trails in your readers. Before long, they'll put your book down because they are being jerked in multiple thematic directions. For example, when I wrote my first book, *Father, Son, and the Other One,* the manuscript was between 50,000 and 60,000 words. My working file actually had 60,000 *more words* in it. So I cut or archived as many words as I used in the final book because those ideas, some of which were good ones, didn't apply to my theme. So test your premise. Can you state it in one simple sentence? If not, then you probably still just have a concept that needs more focus. Your topic should be sustained throughout your book and you need to ruthlessly self-edit unnecessary material out of your project. Now this might not be as true if you're writing a memoir. But the best memoirs I've seen still have a single thematic thread that ties it all together.

• **Structure.** The fun of non-fiction writing is that you get to explicitly spell out your structure in the table of contents. Readers, at a glance, will be able to see your direction from start to end by reading your chapter titles. But each individual chapter should also have its own implicit structure. Your chapters are, in essence, individual narrative units that are taking people on a thematic journey. While there are lots of variations for this (particularly with instructional material like the book you're reading now), I recommend the basic chapter structure of: **Story > Point > Exposition > Story**. So try starting your chapter out with one coherent and clear narrative, then transition that story to one lucid theme or point. You then segue into a few points of application, wrapping it up with one more story that illustrates your central theme. These simple elements will give you a tight, 2,500-word chapter. Additionally, your book chapters should provide three vital elements: the **Know What > So What > and Now What?** You have to give your readers the information they need (**know what**) and you must tell them why that information matters (**so what?**)

and then give them ways to apply that information (**now what?**). Another way to look at this is: **Information** > **Inspiration** > and **Aspiration**. Don't leave out critical **information** that the reader needs to understand what you're talking about. For example, if you tell a story about a time when you were a kid and you then forget to mention that you were a kid, the reader may think, "How old is the author in this story?" Now, instead of reading your awesome illustration and being inspired, that reader has disengaged. Remember, the reader knows *nothing* and you know *everything*. But the story's **information** should serve its **inspiration**. What do you want to inspire people to do? Does the illustration or statistic you're using contribute directly or indirectly to inspiring the reader toward a course of action? And, are you giving them a model or a standard to **aspire** towards? Don't discount the aspirational motivations of your readers. They want excellent (not perfect) models— they want to vicariously live through the subjects in your writing. So let them. View your chapters as individual units that help to tell your overall story or unpack your theme. Organize your nonfiction chapters to help the reader connect the dots. This is an indispensable "law" of good writing.

9. **Get some help.** Seriously, you have to have someone who will be honest with you and has your best interest at heart. I played this role for Kurt when he published his first book, *Epic Grace: Chronicles of a Recovering Idiot.* And Kurt returned the favor when I published my first book. We both needed an objective eye—someone who could serve as a coach and spot all those redundancies and murky sentences and unclear paragraphs and shopworn clichés.

10. **Cut the fluff.** I've received and skimmed a lot of manuscripts that people have sent my way. I usually stop reading after the first page if I see flabby sentences and long unwieldy paragraphs. It tells me the writer isn't self-editing. As writers, we need to thin out the passive voice, excessive modifiers, and vague concepts. Try one simple exercise. Take a paragraph you've written and distill the sentences down to their bare essentials—subject, verb, object. Then go back and add a descriptive word here or there. Next, punch up the prose with an apt metaphor. Make sure your analogies really fit what you're trying to say. Accuracy matters.

Then, purchase a subscription to grammarly.com and check it for spelling and grammatical issues. The building blocks of writing are words, and the supporting struts and beams in the masterpiece you're constructing are tight, descriptive sentences. So pay attention to your underlying sentence structure.

11. **Vary your sentence lengths.** If every sentence is a five-clause whopper then try a few shorter sentences interspersed between them. It's what I call the *"Get it? Got it? Good. Go tell your neighborhood"* principle. In this short paragraph, there are two sentences (interrogatives, "Get it?" and "Got it?") to begin with. One shorter sentence (an adjective, "Good") in the middle and one final longer statement, (an imperative, "Go tell your neighborhood"). Try building succinct paragraphs that vary your sentence lengths and this will help avoid monotony. Also, keep in mind that every paragraph is a mini essay. Do you remember the essay from college or high school? I teach my students in college courses to create a five-paragraph paper. And each of those paragraphs should be broken down with a similar structure: An **Introduction** (topic statement). The **Body** (supporting details). The **Conclusion** (reinforces the original premise of the paragraph). A

Transitional Sentence to the next paragraph (if needed). You may want to identify a favorite author who does this well and try diagraming or dissecting their sentences. With practice, you can create interesting paragraphs with varied sentence lengths.

12. **Turn down the volume.** A sure rookie mistake is to use *lots* of character styles for ***emphasis.*** Keep your writing mostly clean from using lots of italicized words or phrases. Typically, you should only use italicized words for foreign words, words that sound like words (such as "he hit the floor with a *smack*"), or the occasional emphasized word (but please don't overdo it with this). Also, NEVER EVER USE ALL CAPS for emphasis. It is an immediate giveaway that you are a joe not a pro. Additionally, do not end every other sentence with an exclamation mark! Or worse, for additional emphasis, *TWO EXCLAMATION MARKS!!* Or worse *TWO EXCLAMATION MARKS AND QUESTION MARK!!?* If you want your writing voice to be "hot" then write well. Don't try and turn up the heat by adding these amateurish character styles all over the place. The net effect of too much of this is that your writing will look unprofessional. So dial it down and let the quality of your writing create the dynamic range you desire.

13. **Use descriptive language.** More adjectives won't make your writing more effective. But the right adjective(s) can turn a boring sentence around. Start with one solid modifier that aptly describes your subject, then add an alternative adjective if needed. Be careful that your descriptive devices do not create redundancy, but instead add color and texture to your canvas. Also, don't mix up your adverbs and adjectives. We do this in conversational language all the time and sometimes it's okay for conversational effect. An *adverb* is a word (usually ending in *ly*) that modifies a verb, adjectives, and other adverbs. However an *adjective* modifies a substantive—or a noun. So don't confuse adjectives and adverbs. I recommend using thesaurus.com to help you enlarge your vocabulary choices and to identify these critical parts of speech.

14. **Watch your point of view.** This may seem like it is only a problem for fiction writers but nonfiction writers can make this mistake also. Point of view is the perspective of the narrator. You can use first person singular or plural (I, we). Or second person (you), or third person (he, she, it, they). If you narrate a story try to stick with one dominant point of view (for that story). While there are lots of literary works that use multiple points of

view, the degree of difficulty to pull this off in fiction is higher than a singular point of view. With nonfiction, each individual story and illustration can be told from a different point of view, depending on the needs of that particular story.

15. **Be careful not to mix tenses.** I still do this from time to time. I start out telling a story in the past tense (using a simple aorist) and then unconsciously switch over to the present tense. A good example would be something like, "I grew up in rural Virginia. My dad had four hunting dogs that drove me crazy. And it was my job to feed them. I hated having to feed those miserable howling animals. Every day I filled up their bowls with food. I walk up to the dog pen, take the bowls full of food and drop them over the fence. The dogs bawl and bark and I don't care..." Do you see in this short paragraph how I changed from the past to the present? If you missed it, go back, reread it, and see if you can spot when I made this tense shift. When you narrate a story in nonfiction writing, make sure you stick with one tense or the other (for the most part).

16. **Write actively and use the passive voice strategically.** I grew up hearing the occasional snarky English

schoolmarm complain about students' use of the passive voice. The conventional advice is that writers should use the *active* voice where your subject performs the action in the sentence. While this is a good rule of thumb, I want to encourage you to occasionally use the passive voice in a strategic way. Sometimes authors can use the passive voice to better emphasize the object in the sentence. When Thomas Jefferson wrote, "that all men are created equal" he could have stated this in the active voice, "God created all men equal." Instead, the sentence puts the emphasis on the object—*the men* who are created equal. So use the passive voice when it best serves your sentence. Also, on a rare occasion, an author can use the passive voice when no subject is supplied in the sentence. Again, don't overdo it with the passive voice, but sometimes you can use it with great effect and emphasis.

17. **Write when you don't feel like it.** Often, I will have so much going on in my life that I don't have time to write. I have to consciously choose to sit down and just start writing something—anything. This jumpstarts my creativity and before long, I've sat for three hours and written another chapter or worked on a proposal or written another blog (fearlessconversations.net). There

are times when we'll have to write even though we don't feel particularly inspired in that moment.

18. **Create self-imposed deadlines.** If you don't have a deadline imposed by a publisher yet, then learn to impose them on yourself. This is a great habit to get into. Maybe you want to write four blog posts this month. Put the posts, the title, and the topic on your calendar, and this will help you to develop the discipline needed to sustain a book deal. My publisher gave me four months to finish my first book. I put deadlines on my calendar and was able to finish the book on time. But I had to buckle down and be very committed to meeting my own goals.

CONCLUSION

Remember why you started writing? Something you saw, heard or read triggered the desire to put words to paper. Something made you want to collect and codify your thoughts and share them with others some day. Never lose this motivation because writing is work, it's a joy, and sometimes it's a pain. But you are a writer. And if you want to be a published author, you've got to commit yourself to learning the craft.

CHAPTER 4

THE SCOOP ON PUBLISHING

WHEN I (KURT) FIRST STARTED on my publishing journey, I didn't know anything about the editorial process, the publishing timeline, or the things my publisher expected from me. Frankly, I was scared to admit to anyone how little I actually knew about the publishing world. Of course, as a rookie, I was given lots of grace, but I don't like feeling stupid, so I decided to self-educate as much as possible. In this chapter, I'll distill everything I've learned about the publishing process from dozens of books, blogs articles and my own experience.

Here's the first thing you need to know: don't fake it! One of the worst things you can do is act like you know something when in truth you know nothing. Be honest. Ask questions. Google your brains out, but don't pretend.

If you're traditionally published, your publisher should provide you with some guidance as well as a primary point of contact. Due to significant changes in the industry, most of the employees you'll deal with are busy, but don't be afraid to get their help when needed.

If you're self-publishing, many companies (including CreateSpace) provide fee-based support. Find it. Get it. Use it. It will be worth every dime you pay. You may also find assistance in a variety of Facebook author groups or through the blogosphere. I highly recommend you follow these blogs:

booksandsuch.com

authormedia.com

chadrallen.com

Let's unpack some basics on the publishing timeline.

THE TYPICAL PUBLISHING TIMELINE

What I'm about to provide is generally true if you are dealing with a traditional publisher. Of course, things change, and market demands may alter the time period, but the sequence of events is almost always the same.

- Book proposal completion and revamping with your agent: 1-3 months.
- Agent pitch of your proposal to publishing houses: 2 months to 2 years. (Yes, it can take what will seem like forever. Be patient and trust your agent.)
- Contract negotiation: 2-12 weeks.
- Final manuscript submission to the publisher: 1 week to 18 months after signed contract.

- Editorial process by the publisher: 1-3 months (depending on the size of your manuscript and the editorial backlog).
- Author revisions: 1-4 weeks (after editorial revision letter back to the author).
- Galley copies. Sent to author and potential reviewers and endorsers: 3-6 months after author revisions completed (Note: A galley copy of your book is a pre-publication version of your upcoming book. It may be missing the actual cover, photographs, illustrations, and even text that will eventually appear in the final edition. Typically, the bound galleys are not the same size as the published book.)
- Galley corrections back to the publisher: 1-3 weeks after receipt of galleys.
- Book printing: 1-4 weeks after finalization of galleys.
- Books shipped to retail outlets: 1-2 months after sent to the printer.
- Marketing campaign: 2-4 weeks prior to book release and as long as you can afterwards.
- Official book release: 1-2 weeks after book is in stores.

If you're like me, patience is not your forte, and waiting one to two years for the entire publishing process can be excruciating. However, wait you must because unless you're a NY Times bestselling author, the publishing world moves at a glacial pace. Can things go faster? It's possible. But don't count on it.

Let's take a closer look now at the editorial process and some terms you'll need to understand.

THREE STEPS. THREE TERMS.

Once you receive your book contract, you'll have an allotted amount of time in which to submit your manuscript to the publisher. Sometimes they'll want you to provide the complete manuscript before the editorial process begins, but sometimes they'll want it a chapter or section at a time. Regardless of when you give them parts or all of your manuscript, typically every publisher will put your manuscript through: three grueling steps: The macro edit, the line edit, and then the copy edit. Here's how they're different:

- The **macro edit** is a general content edit of your manuscript. Essentially, this stage is the rewriting phase. If it's fiction, your editor will look at the overall plot, characters, POV, the big picture elements and other aspects of your story. If it's a non-fiction book, your editor may point out questions about application or direction or ask you to provide more information. When I wrote *Epic Grace*, I made occasional assumptions about the reader's knowledge, so my editor asked me to clarify and explain certain things in my book. By forcing me to "fill in the blanks" for my readers, he made my book much better (and about 5,000 words longer).

- The **line edit** phase brings out the red ink in full force. At this point your editor will suggest word changes; identify content inconsistencies, discrepancies or redundancies; and address awkward or missing transitions. The line edit will point out where something doesn't add up or make sense. It's also the line editor's task to ensure that your manuscript adheres to the publisher's standards and guidelines. The editor of my first book deleted or replaced some words deemed inappropriate by the publisher.

- The **copy edit** is the final and most detailed edit of your manuscript. This is point at which the grammar police correct punctuation, spelling, typos, and improper word use (e.g. "their" versus "there"). Depending on the publisher, sometimes footnotes are verified and facts checked in this final stage prior to printing.

Again, this is a potentially challenging and painful process for most of us. Writing a book is like having a baby, and nobody wants to hear that his or her baby isn't perfect. Getting my first chapter back from my editor bathed in red ink sent me into a tailspin, but I grew, and my book is better because of it.

One last thing. The editing phase can be long and tedious depending on the quality of your submitted manuscript (some of you have degrees in English, some of us don't), the volume of your manuscript, and the amount of work piled up on your editor's desk. Be patient.

Before we wrap up this chapter, let's take a look at some useful tips on publishing.

TIPS ON TRADITIONAL PUBLISHING

So let's say you've gone through the steps, you've survived the gauntlet of interviews, and the publisher has mailed you a contract that you're ready to sign? Now what? In this section I (Jeff) want to cover some rookie tips on helping you to negotiate that contract and finish that book on time.

Rookie Tip #1: Read before you sign. A good publisher will not want to take advantage of you. However, this is a business not a charity. Your publisher is not a 501(c)3 non-profit organization who exists to help the bedraggled masses with free services and ministries. That's what churches and charities do. Your publishing house is a business. As a business their purpose is to make money. So before you sign that contract you need to read the fine print. Make sure your agent has read the contract and if there are any issues that need to be addressed let your agent go to bat for you. You may, for example, be honored by the fact that your publisher has provided a "first right of refusal" clause. This means they get dibs on your next title. They can choose to pass on your next book, but they get the first shot at your next project. If you don't understand these kinds of clauses make sure you ask the publisher and your agent. As Kurt said earlier, don't pretend like you know something you don't know. Ask.

Rookie Tip #2: Write for the love writing. We mentioned this early on but it needs repeating. Write because you love the craft. Write because you are a writer—because you are wired to do it. Now of course there is nothing wrong with wanting to write as an income stream and many authors do figure out how to translate their published book into paid writing gigs. But my advice is not to sell your house or quit your day job. View writing as your hobby, your passion, your love or your supplemental source of income. Unless you are really lucky or blessed, you likely won't be retiring from the sales of your first book.

Rookie Tip #3: Recheck those deadlines. When you get the contract in hand take a look again at your deadlines. I suggest you put them on your calendar. Then, backfill your calendar with self imposed deadlines to keep you on track. For example,

- Contract signed: Aug 1st.
- Publisher's deadline for manuscript: Feb 1, 2015
- Self imposed deadline:
  - Sept 1, 2014: Ch's 1-4 done.
  - Oct 1, 2014: Ch's 4-8 done.
  - Nov 1, 2014: Ch's 9-12 and epilogue done.
  - Dec 30-Feb 1, 2014: All self-edits, footnotes, consent forms signed and returned.

This schedule may look impossible, but it is very similar to what I did with my first book. I wrote the bulk of that manuscript in just under 90 days, I got all my consent forms, finished the front and back matter, and properly formatted the footnotes. With discipline and determination, you can make your editor very happy by being precise and thorough.

Rookie Tip #4: Stay diligent, teachable and flexible. You will undoubtedly come to points of disagreement with your editor regarding some creative choices in this editing phase. May I recommend that you keep an open mind and remain teachable. My editor, for example, changed one of my chapter titles (one that I particularly liked) and I didn't think hers was as good as mine. With an open heart and in a kind way, I suggested an alternative title to both of ours, and that's the one she went with. I didn't get the original chapter title I wanted, but I got something we could both live with. At the end of the day don't sweat it. You're going to be published so don't let the *prima donna* syndrome derail you in the editing phase. Stay teachable and flexible.

Rookie Tip#5: Your words are not inspired holy writ. If the editor changes a passage or a paragraph or suggests a chapter reorg, don't throw a hissy fit. Ask them why and hear them out. You are not the apostle Paul or Peter and the world is not going to stop turning because a few paragraphs were changed in your manuscript.

Rookie Tip #6: Pay attention to cover art/book design. I was surprised at how much I cared about cover art for my book. My publisher sent me an original galley copy (a PDF proof) with cover art that I thought was completely wrong for the book. I quickly mobilized and lobbied for a better design. Ultimately they were gracious and worked with me and we ended up getting a very nice cover. So, don't be shy. Keep in mind that the answer is always no if you don't ask.

TIPS ON NON-TRADITIONAL PUBLISHING

I (Jeff) started this book out by asserting that you actually don't need this book at all (I know, I've been told I'm quite the salesman). Seriously, if you want to publish your stuff you can start a publishing business and self-publish it like yesterday. You don't need to go the traditional route in order to bring that manuscript to life.

So again, what do you need a publisher for? The traditional publishing house will supply several benefits for you that you wouldn't get otherwise,

- **Industry cred.** A traditionally published book means that a group of professionals in the publishing industry thought your stuff was worth publishing. It was worth their financial risk because they believed there was an audience for your words. Knowledge of this will make you feel soooo good but the truth is you don't need their affirmation. You may want it but you *don't need it* in order to be published.

- **Open doors.** A traditional contract will also open some doors to you that would have been closed. Conferences, speaking engagements, radio interviews, magazine articles, TV spots, book signings—all are a bit easier to come by when you've got a legit traditionally published book out there.

- **Greater readership.** Let's face it. You want to publish because you want people to read your book. Now you may have far more readers of your blog than will ever buy your book. But when it comes to people who buy books (and read them) the vast majority read *traditionally published books.* I know that sounds tight but it's right.

- **Greater distribution.** It's also true that traditional publishers have wider distribution channels (some you have not even thought were possible). So, in terms of the ability to get your book out there in the form ads in magazines, catalogs, libraries and chain stores, the traditional house has the edge.

WHEN TO BYPASS TRADITIONAL PUBLISHING

So, why would you sidestep all this for non-traditional publishing channels? I can think of a few good reasons.

- **Established sales channels.** If you have a ministry, run a seminar, or teach a conference in which you need an immediate, high quality study guide to use with participants, then the self-publishing route may be right for you. Do not discount the power of a simple, elegant study guide. If it looks and feels professional, people are likely to use it and keep it on their shelves. If it looks and feels professional, participants will be more likely to sign up and show up for your course or seminar—especially if they have a chance to sample the goods beforehand. I have firsthand experience with this. Trust me, bring a sweet 100 page study guide to your course or seminar and you will wow your participants and give them something that will not end up in the floorboard of their car.

- **A legacy item.** If you have a life story that you want to pass on to your progeny, and you don't care about the masses or throngs of readers in the marketplace, then indie publishing may be right for you.[8] In one of my mentoring appointments at a recent writer's conference, a participant showed me the autobiography she'd written for her grandchildren. She had self-published it through CreateSpace and it had a beautiful cover, excellent layout and design, and it appeared to be a wonderful story. Her writing was even better than acceptable. She asked me, "Should I seek to get this traditionally published?" I responded, "Why? This is a wonderful gift for your intended audience. Your grandchildren and their grandchildren will know your story and know where

---

[8] indie publishing includes small presses, mid-size independent publishers, university presses, e-book publishers, and self-published authors.

they came from. How wonderful!" She left convinced that she didn't need to traditionally publish it for it to have meaning or purpose.

- **You're in a hurry.** You may have a super book idea and you just can't wait two years for the glacial speed of the publisher. Kurt has several books he's working on right now that may or may not end up being traditionally published and he doesn't have forever (not that he's that old). If you're an author with a lot to say on a range of topics and you want to share it with the world but you want to do it "snap snap" then the traditional route will not work for all your projects.

- **Creative Control.** If you want creative control and want to keep any profit generated by your book, then traditional publishing is not for you. For example, Kurt and I created this book on publishing and are intentionally not shopping it with big publishers. Why? Because we want to get our conference notes in people's hands right away and we want complete creative control over it.

DISPELLING ONE, BIG, FAT MYTH

Now that we've covered this ground, I think it is important to dispel one hellacious myth that we've heard over and over. If you go the traditional route, you'll make money, and it won't cost a cent. But if you go the non-traditional route you'll have to take out a second mortgage on your home.

Wrong.

Both options will cost you. In fact, because of the low obligations of most self-publishing companies, the indie or co-publishing route may even be cheaper. For instance, I was so pumped when my book first (traditionally published) book came out that I bought box loads and began to sell and give them away. Once I went through my initial boxes, I bought more and began to sell and give them away. Also, the publisher, last time I checked, hasn't reimbursed me for my travel costs, or any of the other things I've done to market and promote my traditionally published book. The truth is, I went in the hole to publish my book with a traditional publisher. By contrast I've spent hardly any money publishing my own e-books and non-traditional materials for use in my ministry.

But you better believe that I am motivated in both cases. It just is a myth to think that traditional publishing will result in your living large while non-traditional publishing will leave you penniless.

That said, there are some predatory self-publishing companies out there you'll need to avoid. Again, read the fine print before you sign.

WEIGHING YOUR OPTIONS

You have several non-traditional options available to you. Here are a few to consider along with some reasons why each is worthy of consideration.

Rookie Option #1: A standard self-publishing company. Google the words "self-publishing companies" and you'll be deluged with choices. But you want to make sure you also Google "_____ publishing company complaints." Make sure the self-publishing company you pick is reputable, creates quality products comparable to traditionally published material, and they have good distribution channels. The typical costs for these companies is probably around $3,500-$5,000 to get your book into print. Typically with these companies, you pay an upfront fee which is buying a "package" and they take your manuscript and turn it into a book for you. Depending on which package you purchase, the indie option will at least get you a fairly decent looking book in hand to give to your kids and your family, or to sell through your own distribution channels.

Rookie Option #2: Co-publishing (or Hybrid publishing). Co-publishing is somewhat different than self-publishing. In this model you and the publisher share the costs. Some of the cost is on them and some on you. Typically this option is less expensive and more selective. For example, I had a conversation with Terry Whalin, who at the time was a sales rep for Morgan James.[9] Terry told me that they receive stacks of proposals each year. But they are selective about who they publish, choosing only 150 titles every year. Typically with the co-publishing option, you will pay a flat fee (anywhere from $1,500-#3,500 up front). The publisher carries the rest of the amount for editors, cover design artists, and sales and marketing. This can vary from company to company, so make sure you do your homework before you sign with a co-publisher.

Rookie Option #3: CreateSpace. CreateSpace (CS) is a great option if you need a quality book, study guide, or an informational manual for your organization. If you have a business tax ID number and have set up a business checking account, you can sign up and CS has a range of quality options. When Kurt and I first began our publishing company, Essential Life Press, we basically started it as an imprint (a publishing trade name) of CS. We created the study guides, the artwork, wrote the copy, provided the

---

[9] Morgan James refers to their co-publishing model as "Entrepreneurial Publishing."

editing and managed the distribution and marketing, while CS gave us a snappy digital printer, unbelievable distribution channels, and the best contract structure you could ever ask for. So we were in business for a minimal cost. What's not to like? Next year at this time we will have published nearly a dozen books, study guides, and leadership manuals. Talk about "snap, snap." This is an awesome option if you have a business structure and need a high quality printer and limitless distribution channels.

CONCLUSION

Don't be afraid of these options. Until you land that coveted traditional contract, any one of these non-traditional choices can help grow you as a writer and a marketer. You can and *should* do both.

CHAPTER 5

BULLETPROOF MARKETING

YOUR DREAM HAS COME TRUE! Your book is getting published. The cover design is done. The grueling editing process is finally over. Incredible endorsements are rolling in, and now you get a call from the marketing team at your publishing house.

"Hey, Karen, we're thrilled to represent you and get your book into the hands of people all over the country!"

With a smile as big as Texas and a heart beating double time you say, "That's fantastic! What do you need from me?"

The marketing manager replies, "We'll send you our marketing plan in a day or so and your publicist will be in touch soon."

If you're a rookie, here are your next two thoughts, *I have a publicist . . . how stinkin' cool is that!* And, *Hmmm . . . I wonder what a publicist does?*

Shocked back to the conversation, the last thing you hear is, "We're looking forward to partnering with you to promote and market your book."

Lost in thought, you now ponder, "*Partnering with me*

to promote and market my book..." what exactly does that mean?

THE FIRST HURDLE

Marketing is foreign to most writers. Many of us are baffled by the "M" word, and we have little or no idea what to truly expect from a publisher. What's more, some of us view the marketing of our product as little more than self-promotion, and that seems a bit arrogant. You are well aware that few appreciate pleas of desperation: *Please buy my book!* You're fairly certain your family and friends will buy a copy, but beyond them, you're not sure.

You know that most people hate advertising. In fact, the only time people care about an ad is when there's something in it for them. When someone shows up at your door to sell you something you don't need or want, or sends you spam, how do you feel? Irritated. So the idea of promoting our product creates a tension in many of us.

One of the first realities you will need to embrace is that that marketing not about *you*. Hopefully, you're not marketing your book to become famous but instead you're doing so because you believe it will help, encourage, inspire, or at least entertain your readers. If that's the case, and I trust it is, then marketing is not about self-promotion, but rather about getting a gift into the hands of people who need it. If you don't change your attitude about marketing, you won't succeed. (Go back and read that last line again, or you might as well stop reading this chapter now.)

Even if you have no problem tooting your own horn, you probably are clueless about what it takes to market your book to the masses. All of this marketing and publicity talk can be terribly overwhelming. Don't despair; read on and you'll find some simple steps anyone can follow.

IT'S MORE AND LESS THAN YOU THINK!

About three months before my book released, my publisher's marketing manager sent me the sixteen-page marketing plan. I was so excited I wet myself! It included information regarding sales presentations to big-box retailers like Wal-Mart and Costco. It identified retail chain partners like Barnes & Noble and Target. The plan covered an aggressive blog campaign, trade print publicity plans with publications like the Washington Post, Outreach Magazine, and Guideposts. It even listed radio and TV programs it would send releases and customize pitches to. Most exciting to me, as a speaker, was the statement, "PR will coordinate media interviews around the author's speaking schedule in key cities,"

I told my wife and about fifty friends, "This is going to be awesome!" When I went to bed that night, I dreamed about my guest author appearance on the *Today Show*. In the back of my mind, however, I kept hearing the voice of my writing mentor, "Don't expect the publisher to do squat; you will be the primary marketer of your book, and thirty days after it releases, you will be the only one promoting it."

Sure enough, things did *not* go as expected. To his/her credit, my publicist did get me on an international television program seen by millions and several radio interviews across the country, but after a month or so, I was the only one beating the drum for my book.

In this chapter, I'm going to tell you what you must do before and after the release of your book. The key word in the previous sentence is "you." Even if you have a stellar marketing team and publicist in your corner, they will probably do less than promised. You will need to do a lot more than you think to get the word out, and that's not a bad thing.

WHERE DO I START?

Assuming you've done your homework and you have a compelling book proposal, it's time to pull it out and utilize your bio, the snapshot (aka: elevator pitch), and the benefits section or selling points to develop your book media kit. This material, along with a simple and short cover letter, is your ticket to getting speaking, radio or TV gigs. By the way, be sure to include some suggested interview questions with your media kit.

Every time I speak somewhere or end up on the radio or TV, my book sales bump for several days. You can find email or snail mail addresses for just about any media outlet on the web.

Yes, if you have a publicist,[10] he or she will create this media kit, but you will want a copy in your hands to use *after* your publisher has moved on to their next project. If you don't have or can't get this from your publisher's marketing team, see the sample provided in the appendix to create your own.

Next, develop specific, realistic and attainable goals.

- How many media packets will you send out each week?
- How many follow-up emails or phone calls will you make to radio and TV program directors each month?
- How many social media (Facebook, Twitter, Pinterest, etc.) posts will you make each day? I would suggest you choose only two social media options to focus your

---

[10] I highly recommend Don Otis with Veritas Inc. veritascommunications.com

attention on. Experiment with posting on different platforms for a few months prior to your book launch to see which works best for you.

• At least three months prior to your book release and for at least three months after publication, keep making the contacts and offering to appear whenever and wherever possible.

Marketing is hard work and it takes times. You must be willing to expend the time, energy, money, and effort to succeed. Speaking of work, let's walk through a list of things you will need to do. Don't be snowed under by everything you read here. Start where you can and keep moving forward.

THE BULLETS OF YOUR BULLETPROOF PLAN

• **Develop your own author website and author page on Amazon (authorcentral.amazon.com).** At first, you must focus your marketing on discoverability. You won't sell a single book because of your site if you don't provide a simple way for buyers to do so. Of course, people can go online and search for it on Amazon or Barnes & Noble, but you want to drive traffic to *your* site so you can build a mailing list. Your website will help you develop your tribe. Visiting an author's website is the primary way book readers find out about authors and their books. Be sure to include links to multiple online booksellers who carry your book. If at all possible, provide a free sample chapter of your book on your site as well. If you have no idea how to create a website, it will be worth every penny you spend to hire someone who does.

- **Build your email list.** At first, I viewed book promotion email as an antiquated way to communicate and nothing more than junk mail. I didn't think it mattered. However, the best way for you to connect and stay involved with your tribe is via email. Did you know that typically only 1-3% of your Facebook posts end up on anyone's wall? How Facebook determines who gets what is confusing (their algorithms must be top secret), but even if you posted something every hour of every day, it's not as effective as a single email. Of course, people can mark it as *spam*, but if you're providing something truly worthy of their attention, they will keep opening what you send. If you're not building your email list, then you're missing one of the most effective marketing tools available. There are multiple email subscription services available. I use MailChimp. Furthermore, you will need a feature box on your website that makes subscribing easy. Offer bait to get folks to subscribe. Seth Godin calls this an "ethical bribe," which simply means you are giving them something in exchange for them giving you their email address.

- **Become an expert at using social media.** Create an author fan page on Facebook that promotes you (builds your brand) and a book page that promotes your specific product. Here's the link to set up your fan page: http://www.facebook.com/pages/. This social media site is the one of the largest in the world with over one billion active monthly users. Set up a Twitter and Pinterest account where you can post regular, short excerpts from your book. Find and use shareable (non-copyrighted) pictures with every Tweet or post. People are visual, so draw them in with a great photo. Again, always include a link to your website on everything you post. Here are some other ideas to consider:

- **On Facebook, join as many author and book group sites** as you can, and appropriately promote your book and blog within each group. The idea here is to utilize social media to create a buzz about your book and to drive people to your website. I also use Google+ and LinkedIn, but not as much. See these links for examples of what Jeff and I have done:

www.KurtBubna.com

www.fearlessconversations.net

http://on.fb.me/kurtbubna http://twitter.com/kurtbubna

- **Offer a free giveaway of your book** or something else your readers will enjoy on your social media sites as another great way to create traffic to your website.

- **Create contests** in which readers buy your book or sign up for your blog or newsletter for a chance to win something valuable.

- **Get a professional or good picture taken** of you and use the same image on *all* of your profiles. You are the brand, and you need it to be consistent and recognizable.

- **Consider using Facebook ads.** This is a relatively cheap way to reach a target group defined by you for a set period of time or until you reach your budgeted limit.

- **Recognize that social media is social.** It's not just about electronic advertising. Connect with your followers. Follow them back. Respond to their comments and ask how you can help them. The more reciprocal you are, the more response you will see. Along these lines, be sure always to ask people to share your posts and tweets with *their* friends. Networking starts with your family and friends, progresses to members of your community and your professional acquaintances, and then (hopefully) branches out to people you don't know by asking people to use their network to help yours.

- **Use social media to do a book launch** two to four weeks prior to your release. See the <u>Appendix D</u> for more about this and some sample material.

- **Blog often.** If you want to drive current and new readers to your website and build your mailing list, you will need to provide new and read-worthy content. They won't keep coming back if there's nothing updated for them to see. Once the wow factor of your amazing website wears off, these readers will move on. Entire books have been written about blogging, but here are a few pointers.

- **Blog on a regular and timely basis.** I recommend once a week at least.

- **Create intriguing titles.** In real estate, the mantra is location, location, location. In blogging, it's title, title, and subtitle. You have about two seconds to grab the readers' attention and entice them to open and read your blog. I invest an inordinate amount of time thinking about my blog titles. Why? Because the good ones work and the bad ones don't. Of course, content matters, but if you don't intrigue them with a good title, they'll never get to your amazing content.

- **Write consistent content.** Speaking of content, write content that is consistent with your brand and relevant to your tribe. If you can, write about trending topics and tie your book topic to current popular interests.

- **Tell short stories.** Blogging isn't just about storytelling, but be sure to use short, effective stories to grab their attention or explain a point.

- **Tailor your message.** There's a lot of disagreement regarding the length, but it's somewhere between 500 and 1,000 words. Keep your audience in mind, and write just enough to scratch their itch but not so much that they get bored and unsubscribe.

- **Try to guest post as frequently** as you can on other sites. It is one of the best ways to increase your visibility and draw people to your website. It will help if you offer to trade with bloggers—you write one for them, they write one for you. Many sites can also use what you've written as a blog to post as an article on their website. I write for Pastors.com on a regular basis, but most of what gets published there comes from my blog. Be sure to include a link to your website on every bio used by anyone.

- **Develop a launch team** to create a buzz. Start early. You'll want this team up and running at least two weeks prior to your book release. I strongly suggest you use a survey (try SurveyMonkey.com) to select the team. Offer incentives to recruit team members.

  - An advance reading copy (ARC) of your book (could be an electronic pdf, a spiral-bound paper copy, or an unedited softcover). Readers and writers think its cool to get an ARC!

- A free, signed copy when released.

- Special book related products as a gift(s).

- Your support with their future project.

- Everything they need to promote your book on their social media sites (sample posts, tweets, and pictures).

 - An incentive to the top three participants on your launch team

- **Ask people to write reviews.** The more reviews you have on Amazon or Barnes & Noble, the better. The number of reviews adds credibility, but it also will help sell your book (even if they're not all five star reviews.). People have limited resources, and they don't want to waste even ten bucks on something awful. Start with your friends and family. They probably like you and hopefully they like your book. Ask co-workers, business associates, and neighbors to buy your book and write a review. Some will do so just because they feel valued by you and want to support you. Others will do so simply because you asked. If you don't ask, the answer is always *no*. You can also copy and paste the best reviews on your website and social media sites. The more buzz the better. Important: Don't bribe people to write a review! It's against Amazon's terms of service to offer anything like a discount or gift in exchange for a book review. Amazon can remove your book from its site and ban your account for life (not good!).

- **Do book signings.** Frankly, unless you're famous, book signings don't tend to draw a lot of people, and you might feel like they are a waste of time. However, that bookstore manager or owner might not have ordered *any* of your books to sell if you hadn't connected with him or her. The event also offers you another opportunity to create excitement on your social media sites. The general public thinks it's cool and that you must be on your way to fame and glory to do a book signing. By the way, the local Barnes & Noble sold over two hundred copies of my book. Until I met the manager and offered to do a book signing, they didn't have any available for purchase.

- **Give and it will be given to you.** New York Times bestselling author (and the guy who wrote the Foreword for my first book), Mark Batterson, once told me, "Give away as many books as you can." The idea here is to put your book into a lot of hands as soon as possible because the best marketing in the world is word of mouth. When a friend tells a friend about your book, the book instantly has credibility. If you want something to create lots of interest or even go viral , friends telling friends is the path to success. Of course, for word-of-mouth promotion to work, your book must be worthy of sharing, and if it is, you've now got an army of marketers working for you.

CONCLUSION

Taking personal responsibility for marketing your book matters. Publishers have limited resources and too many books to promote to give their full attention to every author, especially if you're an rookie. Large, traditional publishers simply will not take care of all the marketing and promotion of your book. Don't expect much and you won't be disappointed; sit on your duff expecting them to do everything and you will absolutely regret it. Furthermore, you will learn a lot in the process of self-marketing, and every lesson can be utilized with your next project.

You might have noticed, I didn't cover newspaper or magazine advertising. In my experience, advertising in print media is ineffective. Unless you go big and pay for prime page placement of your ad (which is extremely expensive), yours will be lost in the maze of ads. Think about it: how many product advertisements do you see each day in the newspaper and magazines? And how many of those ads actually drive you to make a purchase?

Don't get discouraged. Keep at it long after your sales numbers start to drop. It's important to continue to market your current book for as long as possible even after you've started writing another. Along those lines, let's finish this book with some helpful input regarding how to survive and thrive as an author. Keep reading.

CHAPTER 6
HELP FROM THE TRENCHES

WE ALL WANT TO SUCCEED. I've never met anyone who aspires to fall short. Of course, we all know failure is a part of life, but we understand the value of getting up, shaking off the dust, and moving forward no matter what happens. But this writing gig is a challenge.

If you haven't figured this out yet, let me be the first to tell you, writing is a struggle. We struggle to,

- Express our thoughts in some intriguing and coherent manner.
- Get an agent.
- Secure a book contract (enduring plenty of rejection along the way).
- Endure the editing process.
- Acquire fabulous endorsements (enduring more rejection).
- Market our masterpiece.
- Plug on when sales aren't quite what we hoped.

And if you love to write, the process continues with your next project as you wonder, "Will this ever get easier?"

The answer is, *no.*

So how do you survive, let alone thrive, in your journey as an author?

FOUR SURVIVAL TIPS

First, decide in advance how you will handle disappointment.

I've never met anyone who likes to be disappointed, and unmet expectation or need is at the heart of all despair. When we want something and we don't get it . . . well, things can get terribly ugly. That being said, it seems that writing and disappointment often go hand in hand.

The first agent I sent my very first book proposal to sent it back with this terse statement, "While I liked the premise and the idea, I confess that the writing didn't win me over." Ouch! Disappointment.

My first book didn't do as well as I had expected it to do. Disappointment.

My first publisher didn't give me a second book deal. Disappointment.

My agent has shopped my book proposal for months and no one's biting yet. Disappointment.

The "D" word is tough to accept and even harder to get past. I know.

The great eighteenth-century poet Alexander Pope

once said, "Blessed is he who expects nothing, for he shall never be disappointed." My first reaction to this high-minded declaration was, "How in blazes can anyone live on planet Earth and 'expect nothing'?; that guy was an idiot!" We all have expectations, which means we all have been let down and hurt. It's vital that you learn how to develop the virtue of tenacity in the face of emotional pain.

I have a note above my computer that reads, "No matter what, keep writing!" Those simple five words inspire me to press on in the face of discouragement. They also remind me that I've *already* determined what I'm going to do when life doesn't go exactly how I planned. I've *already* made a conscious decision regarding the way I'm going to handle the next disappointing news.

You will face times of despair and frustration in your journey as a writer. No one is liked by everyone all the time; deal with it and keep writing.

Second, see failure as an opportunity to grow.
New York Times best-selling author John C. Maxwell wrote: "The difference between average people and achieving

people is their perception of and response to failure."[11] Someone else once said, "When you fail, fail forward." I know we generally want to smack the person who says, "Grin and bear it!", but the truth is many of us grow best in adversity. Someone once said, "Failure is inevitable, but perseverance is optional."

Yes, failure is difficult (and inevitable), but your reaction to failure will make or break you. You typically can't undo what's been done, and going back in time is impossible, but you can determine to *grow* through failure rather than just *go* through it. You can choose your attitude and your next step.

So your book proposal isn't getting any traction with publishers, do you need to rewrite your snapshot or overview? Do your sample chapters need a significant overhaul? Maybe this idea needs to be tabled for now and it's time to work on a different project.

So your amazing book proposal continues to get rejected by traditional publishers, maybe you need to send it to another dozen publishers and burn the pile of rejection

---

[11] John Maxwell, *Failing Forward: Turning Mistakes into Stepping Stones for Success* (Thomas Nelson, 2009), 157.

letters. Maybe you need to go indie or self-publish?[12]

Stephen King received dozens of rejections for his first novel, *Carrie*. One of the publishers sent him a rejection letter with these words: "We are not interested in science fiction which deals with negative utopias. They do not sell."[13]

William Paul Young, my friend and bestselling author, had over fifty publishers reject his book, *The Shack*. He decided to self-publish and sold over eighteen million copies!

So you don't sell enough books to get another dime of royalties, view this as an opportunity to assess your writing, your marketing plan, and maybe even your publisher. We all can grow. In what areas do you need to develop? What can you do better next time? What can you do to continue to build your platform?

Failure doesn't have to be the end of your story—not figuratively or literally. But you must be willing to evaluate ruthlessly and to grow consistently.

---

[12] indie publishing includes small presses, mid-size independent **publishers**, university presses, e-book **publishers**, and self-published authors.

[13] Michelle Kerns, "30 Famous Authors Whose Works Were Rejected" (2009), http://www.examiner.com.

Third, develop a humble heart and a hefty hide.

Disappointment can be discouraging. Failure may not be fatal, but it's still tough to face. Criticism, on the other hand, can be cruel, and even constructive criticism is a thorny rose for most of us.

I wrote this note in my personal journal early in the editing stage of my first book: "What's black and blue and red all over? Answer: A rookie author's manuscript in the hands of a professional editor!" It's not easy when you pour your heart and soul into a manuscript and you get it back butchered with red ink. For any writer, their words are almost holy. *How dare my editor touch the holy grail of my inspired words!* In some ways, it's like having a child and being told that your baby isn't perfect. What the Ford are they talking about?

However, about two weeks into the grueling editing process, it hit me: my editor is making me a better me. I can fight him, or I can decide to sail in this sea of red ink. I chose to raise my jib and sail.

Here are some suggestions that will help you navigate the editing process,

- Be different: Ask for brutal feedback. If you care about the end product don't just endure the editing process, embrace it. Have the heart of a lamb, but the hide of an elephant.

- Take constructive criticism with gratitude not attitude.
- Be careful not to let the editor change your voice, but don't use "I'm guarding my voice" as an excuse for poor writing.
- Take the path of humility because it's the best route to personal and professional growth. Besides, no one likes an jerk.

Lastly, connect to an encouraging community.

Most of us sit for hours alone in front of a computer screen. Lots of us are introverts who prefer to be isolated, and we find ourselves rejuvenated in moments of solitude. Given the choice between hibernating or engaging with others, we typically choose our favorite writing cave without complaint. However, you cannot afford solitary confinement.

Here are some reasons why you need meaningful connections with others:

- Community gives you context. You need the perspective of others.
- Connection provides comfort. You need the support of others.
- Cooperation creates a bond. You need the backing of others.
- Collaboration encourages creativity. You need a team to help you think outside your own head.

At some point, you must step out of your writing bubble and remember you write for real people in the real world. In fact, without this connection, after a while you won't have anything worth writing about. We need each other.

CONCLUSION

Keep writing because you were born to write. Remember, you are not alone in this journey, but to survive and thrive requires the long view and a daily choice to keep going and growing. If writing were easy, anybody could do it. For those who have the gift and stay the course anything is possible. So write on!

Appendix A - Book Proposal Template

Your title goes in the header of the document so that it appears on every page. Page numbers go in the footer so they will be on each page. These are precautions in case the prospective editor separates the pages.

NONFICTION BOOK PROPOSAL:

Include this information on your first page.

TITLE

Your book's title here

Sample Title: "How to Raise Good Kids in a Bad World"

AUTHOR

Your name and book title here

Address

Phone Number

Email address

HOOK

This is a short, punchy paragraph that catches the attention of the reader and draws them immediately into the subject matter of the book and its importance. For example, you could start a parenting book out by saying something like, "For every parent who wants to instill lasting values in their children, *How to Raise Good Kids in a Bad World* offers a creative approach..."
Just make sure this opening statement grabs the reader but do this without hype.

Rookie Mistake: Don't use gimmicks. They rarely work and your editor is more interested in the quality of your writing and the soundness of your concept.

OVERVIEW

This paragraph will give the reader a big picture of where your manuscript is going. Let's take our hypothetical parenting book for example. The paragraph would read something like this: *How to Raise Good Kids* is divided into three sections with twelve chapters total. Section I: The Current Crisis. Section II: The Forgotten Foundation and Section III: The Modern Family

Rookie Mistake: Keep it tight. Don't put all your chapter titles in this overview. Save them for later (see below).

PURPOSE

This paragraph can begin with a rhetorical question that resonates with the intended audience such as "Have you ever been there?" Your next sentence will tell the reader why your book will solve or answer the dilemma raised in your opening sentence(s). Lastly, you'll provide two or three bulleted points giving the purpose of the book.

For example, "There are days when parenting feels like rocket science. We don't feel equipped to handle the ever-increasing complexity of parenting in the digital age. What a relief to discover that the secret to parenting a high-tech, 21st century child is found in ancient principles and pathways. In *How to Raise Good Kids,* author _____ will share vital secrets to bringing up children who have a solid foundation and live by a time-tested code... You will learn critical principles such as,

- Reliance on ancient truths and principles is your starting point.
- Good parenting starts with good parents.
- Successful families live with a mission and avoid mission drift.

- You haven't already blown it; you just need some guidance.

How to Raise Good Kids in a Bad World will help you to discover the principles and habits of successful families and to overcome the challenges…"

Rookie Mistake: If your purpose is vague, then this will be a sign to your publisher that your thinking is fuzzy. Sharpen your purpose statement to a fine point. Zoom in on one problem and solve it. Make sure you offer the reader several bullet points as takeaways.

MARKETING

In this paragraph, you'll begin to lay out your marketing strategy in bullet point form. You'll want to include all *actual* platforms and audiences you've currently developed. This could include courses and seminars you teach, churches and events where you speak, podcasts on your personal website, blog subscribers and followers in social media channels. It can (and should) also include what you *can potentially develop* such as a book launch group, a blog and virtual tour, a list of radio and possible media outlets that you have access to, and anything else you can think of (see chapter four for help on developing this).

Rookie Mistake: Do not make up stuff. If you don't really have access to marketing channels, then don't list them. It's better not to inflate your platform and to be truthful. If you fail because you can't market the book, then take some time and go work on your platform while you burnish that manuscript.

COMPETITION

While you definitely don't want to spend too much time on this, you'll need to list a few *current titles* that directly compete with yours. This will show the publisher that your book can succeed in its target market. Three or four should do.

Rookie Mistake: Don't sell other people's books for them. The purpose of the competition list isn't to make the publisher think those other books are great (they already know that). It's to show that your book actually has an audience and can succeed in a noisy marketplace of ideas.

UNIQUENESS

It's true that there is nothing new under the sun. However, you've got to either have an angle that hasn't gotten much attention, or you've got to have an approach that is somewhat unique. Again, using our hypothetical parenting book, let's create a uniqueness statement:

"The subject of parenting is a proven market. While working on his masters in marriage and family therapy, author _____ discovered that most parenting books offered two extremes... Instead, _____ discovered that the secret to effective parenting in the 21st century is to insulate the family rather than isolate them. This involved rooting children in ancient principles and pathways while teaching them to effectively navigate the pitfalls of a technologically advanced but increasingly isolated culture..."

Rookie Mistake: Never, ever say that your book is the only book ever to address this subject or this topic. Your book needs to have a unique angle, but it needs to fit within a potential niche of books already written on that subject.

ENDORSEMENTS

This part can be tricky. It's sometimes difficult to gain endorsements from other authors if you don't already have a publishing deal. Some authors are very selective about who they will endorse (even if you do get a legit deal). But Kurt and I have found that the answer is always "no" if you don't ask. And it's a numbers game. If you ask 100 authors or influential people for endorsements and you only get a 10% response, then you have 10 solid endorsements. So ask away. Also, realize there is a difference between endorsements and testimonials. An endorsement comes from someone who is published. A testimonial can be anyone who is willing to endorse the material (but don't include your mom, unless she is a published author).

Rookie Mistake: Don't get carried away with trying to get a lot of endorsements up front. You don't need pages of these. It's better to get strategic endorsements. For example, I sent my manuscript on discipleship to one author who responded, "Why do you want my endorsement? I don't publish discipleship books." And he very kindly turned me down. So even if you do get a stack of endorsements, you won't want to confuse your publisher. If it's a parenting book, then get endorsements from people who are influential in that field.

BOOK FORMAT

List the Table of Contents or the proposed format of the book. Using our fictitious parenting book, let's create a format:

INTENDED READERS

Now that you've finished your table , you'll want to address more specifically whom you expect to read and purchase your book. You'll want to include vital statistics such as the following: "The audience for *How to Raise Good Kids* will be parents between the ages of 20 and 45 with a moderate to high-level education…The potential buyers of the book will live in a middle-class household who typically buy the majority of nonfiction books, who have purchased a book on parenting in the last 6 months…"

You also may want to include a secondary audience.

MANUSCRIPT

Tell the publisher how far your manuscript has progressed and how large it will be, and estimate the size of each chapter. For example, "*How to Raise Good Kids in a Bad World* will be a 50,000-word manuscript of which 25,000 words have already been written. Each of the 17 chapters will be geared to the modern attention span…" Your chapters for a book this size would be around 2800-3000 words or something like that. Try to avoid 4,000-5,000 word chapters.

Rookie Mistake: Ideally, you will want to have at least the entire book written even though you will submit only two or three sample chapters at first. I actually lost a deal early on because I didn't have the entire manuscript done by the time I received the contract. So get as much written as you can before you submit it. Even if your publisher wants to rearrange or change your original product, you still will have lots of material from which to draw.

AUTHOR BIO

Give a brief biography of yourself, including your credentials and your work history relevant to this project. Keep it brief but write this as if it's going to be the author bio on the back of your future book.

PUBLISHING CREDITS

List in bullet form any publishing credits you have to date. If you have none, then don't include this section. Everyone has to start somewhere. On that note, you do need to start somewhere—preferably as a blogger or a magazine article writer or maybe even the author of some academic journal articles.

Rookie Mistake: I had self-published several study guides that I used in classes that I teach. I used CreateSpace and was able to publish very high quality study guides to sell in my courses. They were all related to the field I was attempting to publish in via a traditional house. At the time, I was under the impression that a traditional publisher didn't care about my self-published stuff, but that turned out not to be true. One of the publishers I worked with went to our ministry web page and was very impressed by the quality and nature of my material. He remarked to me on the phone that he could see from this that I was able to "write this stuff all day long." Those self-published booklets showed my depth of knowledge and skill with the material. So if you self-publish, take the time to do it right and produce a book or books that you can be proud of.

FUTURE PROJECTS

I can't say enough about this section. I ended up getting my first book deal because I had a title on the "Future Projects" list that one of my prospective publishers was interested in. That title turned out to be my first book even though I was proposing something else at the time. So think through some potential future projects that can serve as a series or as follow-up subjects. Using our fictitious book, *Raising Good Kids in a Busy World,* let's think of what follow-up titles might be possible:

- *Raising Good Boys in a Bad-Boy World.* "Bad-Boys" have been idols of pop-culture for many years. From James Dean in "Rebel Without a Cause" to the characters in

MTV's hit show "Jackass," boys who act like knuckleheads get attention. Most often they get the attention of other boys who look up to these geniuses and revere them as mavericks and trendsetters...

- *Raising Good Girls in a Botox World.* Whatever happened to good old-fashioned virtue? ..."

You can see how having potential follow-up titles may help the publisher to know that you are not a one book wonder, that they could have what my publisher called, "a long monogamous relationship" with the you.

Rookie Mistake: Be careful not to list titles that are not in your area of expertise. If you have no training or background in quantum mechanics, then don't propose a book to solve the problems of cosmology. Stay in your lane and propose books that you actually can write in the future.

CHAPTER SYNOPSIS

There are several reasons why you want to provide a chapter synopsis. First, your publisher will glance at this in order to get an overview of your book and the main idea in each chapter. Second, potential endorsers will want to glance at the synopsis first, and many will read only the entire first three or four chapters and then the rest of the synopsis. So make sure this is tight and brief. You'll want to word this as a thumbnail sketch of your project. Here's the format:

PART 1. SECTION HEADING

1. Chapter Title

One, tight paragraph (two or three sentences at the most) describing the gist (not the grist) of your chapter. Don't share every story you'll tell or every subheading you'll use. Keep it brief, just capturing the essence of that chapter.

INTRODUCTION

After you finish the chapter-by-chapter synopsis, I recommend including only the introduction if it is really compelling. Most introductions are skipped by readers and for good reason. If you can punch it up and make it short and interesting, then by all means include it in your proposal. I would shoot for no more than 1,000-1,500 words on this. A long, tedious introduction will work against you.

SAMPLE CHAPTERS

Here is where you will include two or three complete chapters of your book. Make sure you have more written so that if you are asked for more, you can produce them. The sample chapters will show off your writing skills and hopefully dazzle a prospective publisher.

Rookie Mistake: The biggest mistakes I've seen with authors is they try to get too fancy with their proposals. Bright colors, shiny photo paper, different fonts and spacing, etc. won't improve the package. You need to use a standard academic format which includes a Times New Roman font (or Georgia, Baskerville or Garamond), double spacing (creates a little space in that proposal), and standard Turabian-style headings. Here's a quick reference to how Turabian-style headings work.

CHAPTER TITLE (ALL CAPS)

1st Level Heading (bold and main words capitalized)

First paragraph in normal font, is double-spaced, with no fancy stuff (see chapter 3). Also, do not use two spaces after each period (that is an old academic standard). One space will do fine.

2nd Level Headings (Not bold, main words caps)

3rd Level Headings (Flush Left, Caps main words no bold)

Appendix B - Query Letter

Author: Your Name Here

email

Address

Cell Phone

Dear Associates at _____ Agency:

Opening Paragraph: Your first paragraph should grip the reader and pull them immediately into your book. You can start this paragraph with a compelling quote, a captivating story, or a striking statistic. Use one clarifying sentence to end the paragraph.

Second Paragraph: Speak directly to the reader and transition to the subject of your book. This "turn" can take the form of a question: "Have you ever been there?" Show the reader that you can connect your idea to real emotions that will resonate with your target audience.

Third Paragraph: *Start with the title of your book, subtitle,* and follow it up by telling them how your book will scratch the itch (without using those words) that you just created with the first two paragraphs. You may want to give a brief overview of the scope of your book.

Fourth Paragraph: Give a snapshot of your experience and the ways you've personally witnessed the problem that your book is going to address. Tell the reader who you are, what you do, and why you are the author to write this critical book.

Fifth Paragraph: Give the reader a brief idea of your credentials. Do you have any degrees or teaching experience that will support your claim to being qualified to write this work?

Final Paragraph: Tell the reader about the state of your manuscript. How complete is it? How many words do you project the final book to contain? Then thank them for their time. In all this, keep your tone professional and straightforward. Don't get cute unless you really are super cute.

Sincerely,

_____

Appendix C - Sample Book Launch Invite

Dear _____,

Would you like to be a part of something fun and exciting?

The release of my book *Epic Grace: Chronicles of a Recovering Idiot* is getting very close. It is scheduled to hit the stores in early September. I'm very excited!

Having a book launch team that utilizes social media is a big deal nowadays. The idea is to create a buzz of interest for the book within *your* circle of influence (your friends).

I don't want to assume that you want to help, but if you do, that would be awesome. The benefits to you if you are selected as part of the launch team are as follows:

You will get an *early* free version of the book in PDF form and a free paperback copy when the book is released. (We are still asking the team members to also buy one copy of the book from their favorite retailer to give it away to a friend.)

You will get early access to the drafts of my next book, *Epic Life.* This will give you the opportunity to give me your input regarding direction and content.

You will get my full support on your next social media

project (maybe you have a book in you).

You will have fun interacting with a new group of friends in a closed group on Facebook.

You will have my never-ending thanks and appreciation.

If you'd like to participate, please fill out this very brief survey: http://www.surveymonkey.com/s/P2TS7LD

Based on the answers to the survey, 50 people will be selected to be a part of this fun book launch project. If you are one of the *Fantastic-50*, you will be invited to a closed Facebook group that will provide you *everything* you need to participate.

Even if you decide not to complete the survey, please be praying for this project. I know Jesus wants to use this book to bless many with a radical and freeing view of His love and grace.

Appendix D – Epic Grace Prelaunch Kit

This is the official pre-launch kit. It includes Tweets, Facebook posts, the website and book trailer links, and also links for pre-ordering *Epic Grace* that we ask you to share between now and the book release in September. Each day in August, we will post in the *Epic Grace* Facebook Group what we'd like you to copy and share in Facebook and Twitter for the day. Please feel free to also include this info on your blogs.

PDF BOOK COPY:

You will receive a PDF version of the book via email. Please do not share this with anyone; it is a confidential document and for the launch group only.

OFFICIAL WEBSITE:

Go to http://kurtbubna.com/the-book/ for more details about the book, including endorsements.

BOOK TRAILER:

Go to http://vimeo.com/65748222 for the official book trailer video, which *you can post on your pages on or after August 1ˢᵗ*, but not before, due to copyright restrictions. Thank you!

LINKS FOR ORDERING THE BOOK & WRITING REVIEWS:

Please go to these links and "share," "like," "pin," "tweet," and "Google+" them. When it becomes possible, please also go to each of these sites and write a 5-star review for the book. Thank you!

AMAZON:

http://www.amazon.com/Epic-Grace-Chronicles-Recovering-Idiot/dp/1414385048/ref=sr_1_1?s=books&ie=UTF8&qid=1366238620&sr=1-1&keywords=Epic+Grace+by+Kurt+Bubna

BARNES AND NOBLE:

http://www.barnesandnoble.com/w/epic-grace-kurt-w-bubna/1114918369?ean=9781414385044

CBD:

http://www.christianbook.com/Christian/Books/product?item_no=385044&product_redirect=1&Ntt=385044&item_code=&Ntk=keywords&event=ESRCP

SAMPLE TWEETS:

All of these have been tested to be the correct length as long as you don't have any extra spaces before or after them when you copy & tweet them. ☺

TWEET ON AUGUST 1:

"Everything I am is because of the unbelievable grace of God. His grace is truly epic." #epicgrace kurtbubna.com/the-book

TWEET ON AUGUST 2:

"As a grace magnet, I haven't just *gone* through struggles; I've *grown* through them as well." #epicgrace kurtbubna.com/the-book

TWEET ON AUGUST 3:

"God delights in recrafting our sorrows, failures & missteps into trophies of his epic grace." #epicgrace kurtbubna.com/the-book

SAMPLE FACEBOOK POSTS:

POST ON AUGUST 1:

"Everything I have, everything I am, and every good part of

me exists because of the unbelievable grace of God. His grace is truly epic." #epicgrace http://kurtbubna.com/the-book

POST ON AUGUST 2:

"God has taught me much about how to discover his good purpose in my life. As a grace magnet, I haven't just *gone* through struggles; I've *grown* through them as well." #epicgrace http://kurtbubna.com/the-book

POST ON AUGUST 3:

"God delights in re-crafting our sorrows, failures & missteps into trophies of his epic grace."

#epicgrace http://kurtbubna.com/the-book

Terms You Should Know

Acquisitions Editor – A person responsible for evaluating a book proposal to determine a publisher's potential interest.

Author Bio - A short blurb about you as an author describing three things: 1.) Who you are (including anything unique or unusual), 2.) What credentials you possess for writing the book and 3.) What else you have published (if anything).

Back Cover Copy (BCC): The content found on the backside of a book such as endorsements, the author's bio, and a snapshot of the book including the benefits to a reader.

Blog – A website used to present an author's thoughts and insights; a post of an article on a website.

Book Proposal – A written presentation of a book's topic, marketability and a sample of its contents used to secure a publishing contract (usually between 25-50 pages).

Chapter Synopsis – A brief (usually a three sentence) overview of the main idea within each chapter of your book.

Copy Edit – A detailed proof edit of your manuscript looking for wrong or misspelled words as well as grammatical and syntactical errors.

CreateSpace – A publishing arm of Amazon providing self-publishing services.

eBook – An electronic version of a book.

Endorsement – A short paragraph provided by a published author—usually appearing on the first few pages of your book (see all testimonials).

Galley Copy – A prepublication and pre-proof version of a book often missing the actual cover, photographs, and illustrations used to acquire endorsements or reviews.

Hook – The opening sentence of your query letter or proposal designed to grab the attention of the reader and pull them immediately into your project.

Imprint – A publishing company's trade name (such as Passio for Charisma House or Momentum for Tyndale).

Indie Publishing - Publication by small or independent publishers including self-publishers such as CreateSpace and Essential Life Press.

Launch Team – A group recruited to assist with your book launch (i.e. release) for the purpose of creating a social media and marketing buzz.

Line Edit – A thorough edit of your manuscript checking for inconsistencies, discrepancies or redundancies as well as suggesting alternative word use; the second edit in the editing process.

Literary Agent – A person contracted to represent you and present your book proposal to potential publishers.

Macro Edit – A general content edit of your manuscript; the first edit in the editing process.

Mailchimp – A service provided to facilitate the mass distribution of emails or newsletters.

Manuscript – An author's original text in a pre-published format.

Marketing Plan – A detailed strategy for the promotion of a book to media outlets.

Media Kit – A set of material sent to media outlets that includes the author's bio, a brief description of the book, potential interview questions and a copy of the book for review.

Narrative prose – In a non-fiction book, this includes

narrative elements such as stories used to create worlds or pictures in people's minds that make cold principles come to life.

Platform – The email and social media contacts available and used by an author to market his or her books.

Publicist – Someone who represents an author to media outlets in an attempt to get publicity.

Publisher – A company who acquires, produces and markets books.

Publishing Credits – A list of an author's traditional or self-published books, magazine or journal articles, or posts on high volume blogs written within the past two years.

Query Letter – An initial letter sent to an agent presenting you're a snapshot of your book, author bio, publishing credits, as well as the state of your manuscript.

Social Media – Online services (such as Facebook and Twitter) used to connect people.

Testimonial – A short sentence or paragraph endorsement of your book written by a non-published person.

Traditional Publishing – Having a book published by a

standard publishing company.

Tribe – A group of people who belong to your platform and connected to you in some meaningful way.

URL – An acronym for Uniform Resource Locator; the address of a website on the internet.

Voice – The unique and individual writing style of an author.

Writer – A peculiar person capable of transforming caffeine into books.

About the Authors

Kurt W. Bubna published his first book, *Epic Grace ~ Chronicles of a Recovering Idiot*, with Tyndale in 2013. He is an active blogger, itinerate speaker, regular radio and television personality, and the Sr. Pastor of Eastpoint Church in Spokane Valley, Washington.

Jeff Scott Kennedy published his first book, *Father, Son, and the Other One: Experiencing the Holy Spirit as a Transforming, Empowering Reality* with Passio: Charisma House in 2014. He is the executive pastor of discipleship at Eastpoint Church in Spokane Valley, Washington and an Adjunct Professor for Liberty University's School of Divinity and Moody Bible Institute's College of Distance Learning.

About Essential Life Press

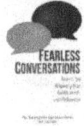

For more books and study guides by Essential Life Press, go to http://essentialifepress.org/